The Great English Walk

Volume One: Chepstow to Hathersage

Margaret and Brian Nightingale

The Great English Walk
1st Edition

Published by
Nightingale Publications
23 Grange Road, BIDDULPH, Staffordshire Moorlands ST8 7SB

Printed and Typeset in Great Britain by
Vibrant Graphics Limited
Radnor Works, 5 Back Lane, CONGLETON, Cheshire CW12 4PP

A British catalogue record for this book is available from the British Library.

ISBN for complete set of 2 volumes: 0 9529490 0 8
ISBN for this volume: 0 9529490 1 6

Front cover: Crews Hill
Back cover: Eagle Rock

Volume 2 (Hathersage to Berwick-upon-Tweed) will be available mid-1997.

Copies of this book and Volume 2 (when available) may be obtained from
Nightingale Publications, 23 Grange Road, BIDDULPH, Staffordshire Moorlands ST8 7SB.

The book is dedicated to all our friends
who have offered us encouragement.

The Country Code

- Enjoy the countryside and respect its life and work

- Guard against all risk of fire

- Fasten all gates

- Keep dogs on leads and under close control at all times

- Keep to public paths across farmland

- Use gates and stiles to cross farmland

- Leave livestock, crops and machinery alone

- Take your litter home, or carry to the nearest disposal point

- Help to keep all water clean

- Protect wildlife, plants and trees

- Take special care when walking on, or crossing roads

- Make no unnecessary noise

Contents

Note: The following sections are only a suggestion. Please do sort out for yourselves what mileage suits you, and do less (or more) according to your capabilities. A facility list at the end of the book gives ideas of where you could break the mileage differently.

GEW Route Map

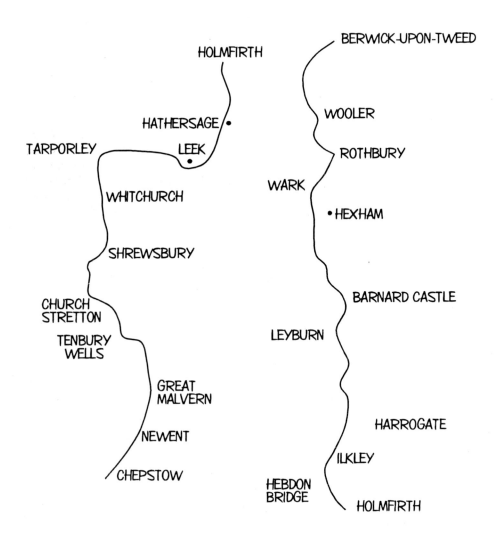

Introduction

WHY?

Having walked most of the long distance paths in the north of Britain, it has long been a dream to establish an alternative south to north, and west to east, path in the UK. The three main existing south-to-north routes – the Pennine Way, Offa's Dyke and the West Highland Way – together with the two west-to-east routes – the Coast to Coast and the Southern Upland Way – are all deservedly very popular, but this route offers something different. A route from Chepstow at the southeast end of Wales, to Berwick-upon-Tweed, almost at the southeast end of Scotland, offers both a south-to-north route and at the same time a west-to-east route. The route is not a straight line between the two ends, but is designed to bypass the Midland conurbations, then swing east round the north of Stoke, in order to continue north again.

There are some 140,000 miles of public rights of way in England and Wales. This walk uses some 600-odd miles of these footpaths to explore some of the best scenery that England has to offer. The really dedicated walker could add on the Southwest Peninsula and Severn Ways to get from Land's End, and then devise a route from the border just north of Berwick all the way to John o' Groats!

The only name for the walk had to be *The Great English Walk* (or GEW). We hope that, in time, the walk will become recognised as an official long distance walk and signposted throughout. The only appropriate sign seems to be that great English emblem – the *OAK LEAF*.

PERSONAL

The description of the walk is as we found it in 1996, and to some extent is a personal record of our journey. The text has been written in the third person for ease of reading. The first 200 miles of the route were walked in one go, with stops at Bed & Breakfast establishments. The rest of the first volume was a case of driving car to a section's north end, leave a bike with a friendly shopkeeper or inn, drive to the southern end of the section and leave the car, walk the section, pick up the bike, Brian then cycled back on a road to the car, and then drove back to the north end to pick up Margaret.

MAPS GENERAL

The only maps produced by the Ordnance Survey showing paths in detail (and easy to obtain) are the *Pathfinder 1:25,000*. It is

The Oak Leaf – The GEW Symbol

expensive to equip yourself with a full set of required Pathfinders, but fortunately the OS now produce a series of *Leisure 1:25,000* maps which cover the ground of quite a few Pathfinder maps. A new range of *Explorer 1:25,000* maps is also now becoming available, and it is hoped that, in time, these will cover all the route.

MAPS IN BOOK

All maps in this book are 1:25,000 (or 2.5 inches to one mile). North is always to the *top* of the page maps. The maps are reproduced from Ordnance Survey 1:25,000 mapping with the permission of the Controller of HMSO ©Crown Copyright, 85793M06/96.

SYMBOLS USED

Many guide books are written showing whether the walk follows a hedge, fence or stone wall, but in our experience these usually clutter the map – and do change! Therefore hedges, stiles, steps, gates etc are not usually shown. There was a television programme many years ago where a farmer with land on the Pennine Way was interviewed. He said *"I'm fed up with all these walkers. Wainwright said go through the gate painted white – I've foxed'em, I've painted it red!"* That is why the maps have been kept relatively simple.

ACCOMMODATION

Walkers' preferences vary, from hotels to guest houses to camping. We have found that the best way to obtain accommodation is to use the Ramblers Association yearbook list of B&Bs, supplemented with contacting Tourist Information Centres along the route.

TOURIST INFORMATION OFFICES

The following is a list of offices on, or near, the route together with telephone numbers –

Alnwick	(01665) 510665
Ashbourne	(01335) 343666
Bakewell	(01629) 813227
Barnard Castle	(01833) 690909
Berwick-upon-Tweed	(01289) 330733
Chepstow	(01291) 623772
Chester	(01244) 317962
Church Stretton	(01694) 723133
Congleton	(01260) 298243
Halifax	(01422) 368725
Haworth	(01535) 642329
Hebdon Bridge	(01422) 843831
Hexham	(01434) 605225
Holmfirth	(01484) 687603
Ilkley	(01943) 602319
Ledbury	(01531) 636147
Leek	(01538) 381000
Leyburn	(01969) 623069
Malvern	(01684) 892289
Much Wenlock	(01952) 727679
Newent	(01531) 822145
Pateley Bridge	(01423) 711147
Rothbury	(01669) 620887
Shrewsbury	(01743) 350761
Skipton	(01756) 792809
Stanhope	(01388) 527650
Tenbury Wells summer only	(01584) 810136
if closed ring	(01568) 616460
Whitchurch	(01948) 664577
Wooler	(01668) 281602

TIMING

We have found that on a day's walk the average pace is about two miles (3.25 kilometres) per hour. This will include time to 'stand and stare', for morning/afternoon breaks and a picnic lunch.

DISTANCES

Most people still think in yards and miles, but metres and kilometres will eventually take over. Walking 100 metres or 100 yards along a road to a stile is really no different, but miles and kilometres are vastly different. In the text distances are given in metres, but on the route maps the indication is shown in miles. NB one kilometre is five-eighths of a mile, and one mile is 1.6 km (or at least they were when we went to school!).

ORDNANCE SURVEY

Maps seem to be updated about every 20 years, so where a post office is marked is no guarantee that it is still there (but there are still some 19,000 in the UK!). Also, you will find that some hedges shown on the maps have disappeared or some arrived!

BOTANY

Apart from the sheer joy of being out in the countryside, an enormous number of walkers now have some interest in identifying plant species (ie. herbaceous and tree species). There are some 8,500 species to be found in the UK, so the argument for becoming a botanist, as well as a rambler, is quite strong.

Many species restrict themselves to the coast or inland only. Again, whilst many species will be found throughout the walk there are many which will only be found in the south, or only in the north. Happy hunting.

HEDGES

You may recall mathematical laws from years ago. Well, Dr Max Hooper invented *Hooper's Rule*. The rule is basically that a hedge can be approximately dated from the number of tree

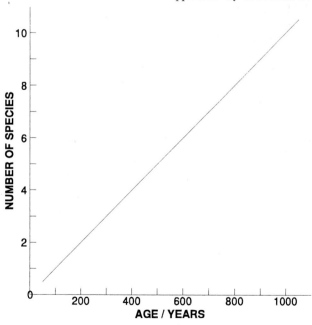

Hooper's Law

species in a given distance. Count the number of native species in a 30 yard (or 30 metre) stretch, and consult the chart to find the approximate age when the hedge was first planted.

The trees (or shrubs) which qualify as old native species are Alder, Apple, Ash, Beech, Blackthorn, Briar (Dog and Field Rose count as two), Broom, Buckthorn, Cherry, Cherry Plum, Dogwood, Elder, Elm, Gorse, Guelder Rose, Hawthorn, Hazel, Holly, Hornbeam, Common Lime, Small Leaved Lime, Field Maple, Oak (pedunculate and sessile), Scots Pine, Plum, Poplar, Wild Privet, Rowan, Sallow, Service, Spindle, Sycamore, Wayfaring Tree, Whitebeam, Willow (white, crack and goat), and Yew.

Identifying hedge ages should give you something to do if you want to add a bit of fun.

LONG DISTANCE PATHS

Along its length the GEW meets the Offa's Dyke Path, Wye Valley Way, Shropshire Way, Cestrian Link Walk, Jubilee Way, Staffordshire Way, Sandstone Trail, Mow Cop Trail, Limestone Way, Worcestershire Way, Coast to Coast Path, Reivers Way, Peakland Way, Calderdale Way, Kirklees Way, Weardale Way, Yoredale Way, Ebor Way, Dales Way, Nidderdale Way, and Pennine Way – but not necessarily in that order – and no doubt a number of others also!

HISTORY

Many years ago, when England was made up of a number of Kingdoms like Wessex, Mercia and Northumbria, the Northumbria King, Aethelfrith, came as far south as Chester to win a battle in AD 616. He must have travelled much the same route as this walk from Northumbria towards Chester.

Years later in the wars against the Welsh, England built castles at such places as Chepstow, Hereford, Ludlow and Chester. This walk therefore could almost be called 'A Royal Route'.

Much later again, as the Industrial Revolution arrived, many canals were built, and these were followed in turn by railways. The canals and railways were the means to open the country to trade and easier access. Both are given just mention as they are met and crossed on the route.

The oldest building still surviving in most villages and towns is the church. The church usually has all the recorded history and the oldest relics in the area and is an extremely important link with our past.

DISCLAIMER

Things do change. The route described is, as far as is known, all on official rights of way, concessionary or permitted paths. Every effort has been made to ensure the accuracy of the walk, but no responsibility can be accepted for any errors or omissions, or changes to the line of rights of way or concessionary/permitted paths. Walkers should always be aware that adverse weather conditions may make some paths impassable with safety, and should always exercise discretion. County Councils are normally the authority responsible for the maintenance of highways, although some Unitary or Local Authorities have taken on this responsibility. A Public Right of Way (or PROW) is a right of passage just the same as a road, and many Acts of Parliament have been passed over the years to give protection to PROWs. The main Acts date from about 1948 to 1952. The main protection at present for PROWs is probably the Highways Act of 1980.

With so many miles of PROWs it is not surprising that there are some problem paths. The major problems on the route are described in the text (with temporary alternative routes where appropriate), and have been reported to the relevant Highway Authority. Hopefully some of the existing problems may have been solved by the time you do the walk. County Councils only seem to respond to complaints, so do report any problems you find to the relevant County Council.

THE ROUTE

The GEW starts at Chepstow, then goes north (certainly not directly) via the Forest of Dean, Malvern Hills, Brown Clee, Wenlock Edge, Caer Caradoc, Shrewsbury, Grinshill, Bickerton Hill, Peckforton Hill, Cheshire Plain, Congleton Edge, Biddulph Moor, Staffordshire Moorlands, Bakewell, Curbar Edge, Hathersage, Derwent Edge, Langsett, Holmfirth, Hebden Bridge, Haworth, Ilkley Moor, Nidderdale, Leyburn, Barnard Castle, Stanhope, Allendale, Housesteads, Wark, Rothbury, and Wooler to Berwick-upon-Tweed.

Norway Maple in Flower

Jacob's Sheep

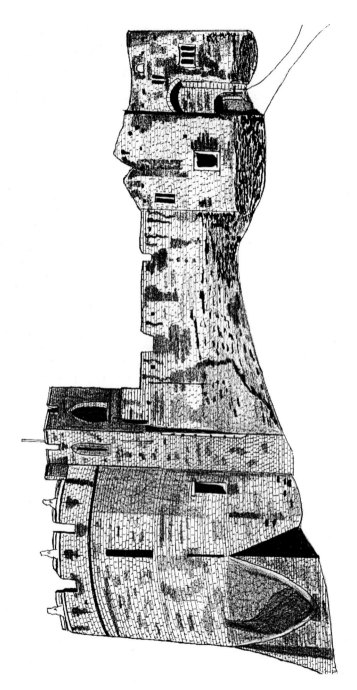

Chepstow Castle

ONE
Chepstow - Viney Hill
(18.5 miles or 29.6 km)

The official starting point of the *Great English Walk* is where the approach road from the castle meets the car park. From here it is a matter of walking past the Tourist Information Centre and the museum, onto Bridge Street, then turning left and going to the old bridge over the River Wye. The boundary between Wales and England is in the centre of the bridge and marked with a plaque. This is some 260 metres from the start point so, sorry, the GEW isn't entirely in England. But you can hardly start a walk in the middle of a bridge! Hence the walk starts in Chepstow.

You cannot leave Chepstow, having just arrived, without a look at its delights. There is evidence of Iron Age and Roman settlements nearby. In Saxon days the place was called *Chepestowe* which means "a market town". The Normans really built the town; William Fitz Osbern began to build the castle in 1067 as a base for the Norman conquest of southeast Wales. At that time the town was called by its Welsh name of Striguil and was known by this name until the 14th century, but today it is the English name which has survived. The castle was the first stone-built castle in Wales, and was greatly enlarged in the 12th and 13th centuries with better walls and with gatehouses and barbicans. Large sections of this work still remain today and the castle has the earliest surviving stone keep in Britain. The castle was so massive that it continued in use until 1690 when it was adapted for cannon and muskets after an epic Civil war siege.

The castle played no part in the wars between the Welsh and English, but in the English Civil War it was held by Royalists until they surrendered in 1645 – an exhibition in the castle explains the reasons behind the war. The whole castle is well worth a visit before embarking on the Great Walk.

As well as building the castle, William Fitz Osbern also brought Benedictine monks from the abbey in Cormeilles in Normandy in 1071 to found the parish and priory church of St Mary. The priory was dissolved by order of Henry VIII in the change to Protestantism in 1536.

Chepstow is mainly medieval. A bridge was built over the River Wye in the 13th century, but the present iron bridge was designed by John Rennie in 1814 and opened on the 24th July 1816 (it cost £20,000 to build).

Possibly one of the biggest events in recent times to affect the town was the coming of the railway. The railway bridge over the Wye was designed by Isambard Kingdom Brunel and opened in July 1852. At the site chosen for the bridge there is a limestone cliff to the east (Gloucestershire) at a height of 40 metres, but the opposite bank (what was Monmouthshire) slopes gently. Brunel's bridge had a main span of 100 metres with three approach spans of 30 metres each on the west side. The foundation cylinders were among the first in the country to be sunk using compressed air. The design, however, was not suitable for high speed trains and, when the girders suffered extensive corrosion, the opportunity was taken to partially replace the bridge in 1962. On the subject of bridges, the A48 road bridge opened in 1988, the first Severn bridge in 1966 and the second

Severn bridge in 1996 (the Severn railway tunnel opened in 1886).

The town itself has many interesting parts. Near the town centre is Beaufort Square, with a gun taken from a captured German submarine in the First World War. It was presented as a memorial to Chepstow's Victoria Cross winner, William Charles William, a seaman killed at Gallipoli.

Bringing your mind back to the present, what about starting the walk? Having arrived at the centre of the bridge over the Wye you now enter England, and more specifically Gloucestershire. The first record of the name was in 1016, some time after shires first came into use. The name then was *Gleawe Ceastre Scire* (which is probably pronounced the same as at present!). Once you have reached the English side of the bridge continue on the same line up the steep lane opposite (with a metal handrail). You meet The Offa's Dyke Path halfway up the lane which keeps you company for the next 350 metres. At the top of the lane cross the road into Tutshill and onto Mopla Road.

Continue climbing up this road as it bends right (and the Offa's Dyke Path goes off to the left), until you reach the junction with the B4228 road.
T h e

road you have come along is the old road down to the Wye Bridge. Turn left along the B4228, onto the pavement opposite and then turn right at Elm Road (which is blocked off for vehicles). After 30 metres turn left along a footpath between houses to emerge over a stile into fields. You now have views of the River Severn for many miles as you walk along. Cross the first field to a kissing gate and a
p a t h

across a long field to the lane at the far right side. Cross the lane and head half-right across the field to a gap in the hedge. Cross through and across a field to a stile at the left side of Bishton Farm, then onto a farm track. Turn left up the track. When the track turns left, carry on into a field. Keep to the right hedge. Don't cross the stile at the end into a lane, but turn left in the field and walk parallel to the lane. Half way across the field go through a gate on your right onto the lane. Turn left.

The banks are full of Garlic Mustard, Cow Parsley, Greater Stitchwort, Hazel, Yellow Archangel, Hogweed, Cleavers, Dog Rose, Rowan, Honeysuckle and Ivy to name just a few species. Cross the old railway bridge,

Boughspring

3

Cross Hill

2

Tidenham

B4228

Tutshill

A48

Castle

CHEPSTOW
GR ST 535 942

RIVER WYE

part of the disused Wye Valley Railway. Passenger services were withdrawn on 5th January 1959 due to a loss of £13,000 pa, and freight ceased in 1964 – except to Tidenham Quarry which produced a particularly hard Dolomitic limestone that was ideal for rail ballast.

30 metres on the right go over a stile into a Larch plantation. Turn left over a second stile. The bund (large embankment) to your right is to shield the quarry sight and noise. The trees change to Beech. At a path junction turn right to go around the quarry. This is a surprisingly delightful walk. After a while the path turns right again at a barn, then left behind the barn. There is now an old estate walled garden to your left. The church of St Mary and St Peter at Tidenham now comes into view. Go over a stile into a track, then another stile and turn left to reach the church entrance.

The first church was probably built at the end of the 10th century and was partially destroyed in 1049 when the Welsh King Griffin burnt Tidenham, but was rebuilt and mentioned in the *Domesday Book* in 1086. The present church was built by Henry Woodyer, who also built the church of St Luke in Tutshill in 1853. Tidenham is yet another place of changed name – the first recording being *Dyddanhame* in 956, which means "Dydda's water meadow". The writer Thackaray visited the village in 1842 and referred to an old rus- tic who had

been *"one of Nelson's veterans"*. In fact, a number of inhabitants had fought in the Napoleonic war – one was an admiral, anoth- er had ridden in the battle of Waterloo, and one had even fought with Clive in India.

There is a horse mounting block at the church. Go through the Lych gate and through the churchyard to the back of the church to find a gate into an old lane (with a wall to the left). Soon high walls are on both sides, before you emerge onto a road. Turn left and follow the road to a slight bend where you go right onto a footpath. Keep a house wall on the left, then head across the field on the same contour. There are great views of the Severn from here. Go over a stile and then keep the hedge on your right. On the same contour go right of a barn to find a stile in the field corner. The path begins to drop towards a hollow, but go over a stile on the left and bear half-right across a 'lawn' to the right of houses and onto a lane.

Turn left on the lane for the climb past the houses of Boughspring. The climb brings you to a left bend – ignore the path to the right – and take the path almost opposite through a wooded glade into fields. Follow the route over stiles – the path then enters a Gorse thicket. Follow the old fence line to the left and enter Parson's allotment wood. Soon the path branches – take the one half-right through a young plantation to meet a wide track at right angles – cross this and carry

River Wye Bridge

on the same line. Another path joins from the right and then after a few metres the track splits again. Take the right split and head for a house. Go over a stile onto a lane. Go along the lane opposite (Kelly's Lane) and pass the side of Ash Grove house. Wild Strawberries, Wood Avens, Common Dog Violet and Dog's Mercury abound. At the bottom of the hill, as the road bends slightly right, take the path on the right into Ridley Bottom Nature Reserve (Gloucestershire Wildlife Trust).

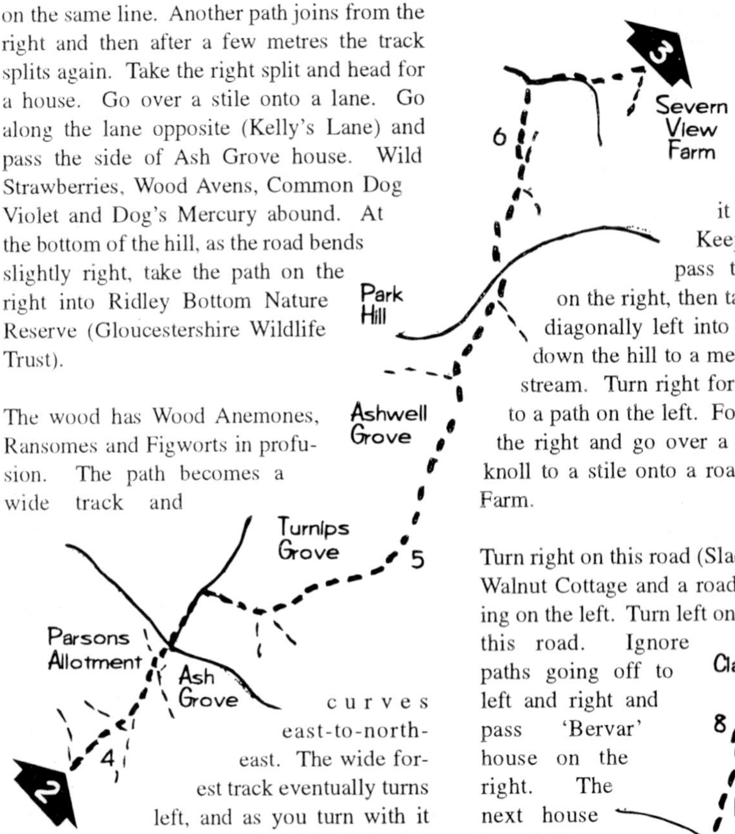

The wood has Wood Anemones, Ransomes and Figworts in profusion. The path becomes a wide track and

curves east-to-north-east. The wide forest track eventually turns left, and as you turn with it look out for a side track to the right. Take this track and ignore forks to both the left and right. A stile on your right carries another path eastwards, but ignore this and carry on the little used (and overgrown) path. Just to the right of the track can be seen a large field – as you get level with about halfway across this field a stile brings a path from the field into the wood. This is your cue to turn half-left and go up a very indistinct incline and climb up to a minor road. The incline is very difficult to negotiate due to undergrowth, but hopefully will improve with usage. There is a signpost on the road, and opposite is a track with the

name Park Hill Common. Cross the road and take the metalled track. Go past several houses, then bear right as it enters woodland. Keep on this track to pass two more houses on the right, then take the path going diagonally left into woodland. Drop down the hill to a metalled track near a stream. Turn right for some 200 metres to a path on the left. Follow the hedge on the right and go over a stream and small knoll to a stile onto a road at Severn View Farm.

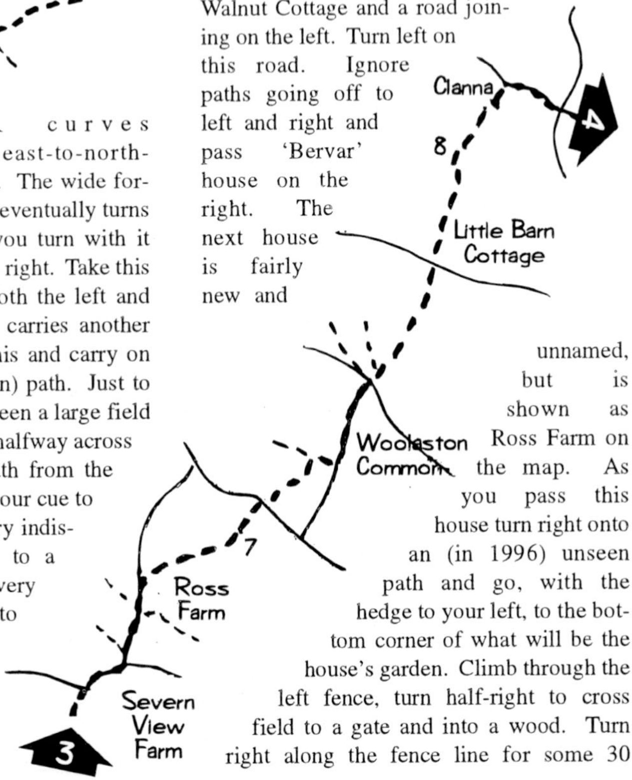

Turn right on this road (Slade Road) to Walnut Cottage and a road joining on the left. Turn left on this road. Ignore paths going off to left and right and pass 'Bervar' house on the right. The next house is fairly new and unnamed, but is shown as Ross Farm on the map. As you pass this house turn right onto an (in 1996) unseen path and go, with the hedge to your left, to the bottom corner of what will be the house's garden. Climb through the left fence, turn half-right to cross field to a gate and into a wood. Turn right along the fence line for some 30

Map labels: Severn View Farm · 6 · Park Hill · Ashwell Grove · Turnips Grove · 5 · Parsons Allotment · Ash Grove · 4 · 2 · 3 · Clanna · 8 · Little Barn Cottage · Woolaston Common · 7 · Ross Farm · Severn View Farm · 3

metres, then left into trees and over a stream into a field. Climb the field about 30 metres to the left of the right hedge. Cross a fence and then a gate onto a road. This is a difficult section in 1996 from Ross Farm, but you have now arrived at Woolaston Woodside.

Cross the road and go up the drive of Badgers Hollow house. At the house take the gate to the left of the drive 'roundabout' and cross through the orchard to a hedge at the rear. Turn right here and then left at the field-end into a green lane and onto Common Wood Lane. Turn right for a few metres to a T-junction and left onto 'Sand Tumps'. Go along to another T-junction with Woolaston Common. Go straight across onto a path in a narrow passage to a stream, and then follow the fence to your right in a field to reach a lane and Little Barn cottage.

Cross the lane and keep on same direction, into beautiful woods. Pass a farm to the left and cross a clapper bridge to climb a bank. Then turn left onto a track to Home Farm and Clanna. Continue on a track to pass Clanna Gardens and arrive at a road. Turn right to a junction and take the path opposite to go diagonally left across the field, to cross a stile and kissing gate. Then to the far left of next field cross over a stile, then another on the left and follow the right hedge (toward Alvington). Pass Park Farm and follow the stiles to a farm track to Nupend and a road. Turn left for 25 metres, then leave road

over left stile and head across the middle of field through a gate. Follow the hedge/fence on the left to the drive of Brook cottage before passing more houses to reach Sandford Road. Turn right down the road to pass houses, then just after the last 'angled' house row turn left on the path up to Sandford Terrace and over the stile at the rear into a field.

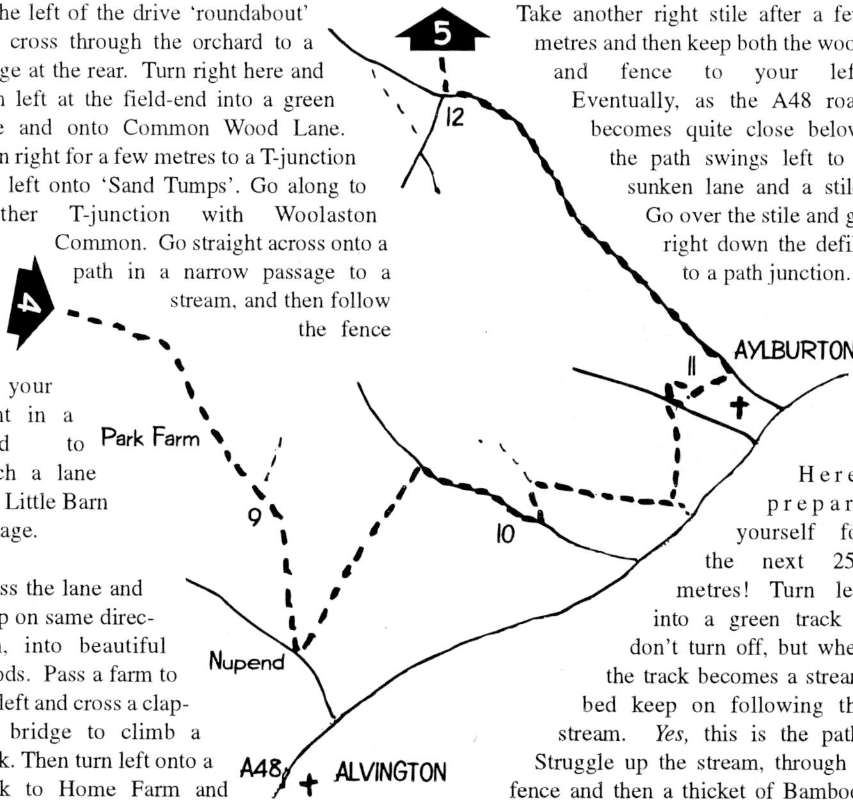

Take another right stile after a few metres and then keep both the wood and fence to your left. Eventually, as the A48 road becomes quite close below, the path swings left to a sunken lane and a stile. Go over the stile and go right down the defile to a path junction.

Here, prepare yourself for the next 250 metres! Turn left into a green track – don't turn off, but when the track becomes a stream bed keep on following the stream. *Yes,* this is the path. Struggle up the stream, through a fence and then a thicket of Bamboo. Scramble up a short, loose banking onto a road (definitely jungle country). Go up the metalled drive opposite to a junction, then turn right along 'The Gables' drive and pass'Pen y Bryn'. Go through a gate to the right rear of a garage into a field and diagonally down the field onto Church Road. The centre of Aylburton village is 200 metres right (first record *Ailbricton* in 1307). Although it cannot be seen from Aylburton, across the

Map labels: 5, 12, 4, Park Farm, 9, Nupend, A48, ALVINGTON, 10, AYLBURTON, 11

Severn some 7 km to the east lies Berkeley Castle. The castle hides the secret of King Edward II's murder on the orders of his Queen Isabella and her lover Roger Mortimer in 1327. The castle was built in 1153 by Lord Maurice Berkeley and has been the home of the Berkeley family ever since. A number of locations around the world are named after the family, .including Berkeley square in London, where our namesake – the Nightingale – is supposed to sing!

A visit to Lydney Castle and the laid out forest walks would be nice, but this is private land without public access (although permission can be obtained from the estate manager for a private visit). The walk must therefore now turn up Church Road for 1.3 km until you reach the first minor road going off to the left. At this point turn right onto a forest track into Lower Old Bargains Wood – there must have been a reason for this name, now lost in the mist of time! The track splits as soon as

the wood is entered – take the right fork and, when it splits again, still keep to the right fork. The wood is fortunately of broad leaved trees, not the imported conifers. After what seems an age, but is in reality only a kilometre, you see a green field through thinning trees to the right. At this point go right on the track to stepping stones over Stockwell brook and climb the track with the field now on your left. When the field ends look for a stile into the top end of the field. Go through two fields until you are level with Chelfridge House, then over a stile on your right into the forest again.

Immediately you enter the trees there are the remains of two limekilns. Go round the kilns to their right and climb to the footpath behind. Climb this old track to meet a larger track coming from your left. Turn right onto this wide track through the broad leaved wood. You are now in the area known as the Scowles.

The River Lye

In 1780 George Wyrall, a local antiquarian, wrote on the ancient ironworks in the forest. He said *"There are, deep in the earth, vast caverns scooped out by mens hands, large as the aisles of churches, and on its surface are extensive labyrinths worked among the rocks and now long since overgrown with woods. They certainly were the toil of many centuries, and this perhaps before they thought of searching in the bowels of the earth for their ore – wither however, they at length naturally pursued the veins, as they found them to be*

wood. The path is not that distinct, but should not be a problem to follow. After almost a kilometre you reach a minor road (Brookhollands hamlet is to the left). Cross the road and onto the drive to Tufts fish farm, with Tufts brook to the left. After 50 metres go over stile on the right, and follow the path as it climbs and bends to the right to reveal the fish farm down in a dip below. When you meet a wider path, cross over on the same line and contour until you meet a wide forest road joining from the right. Go left along this for 50 metres, then take track on the left diagonally down to the rail line. Cross the line then turn right along, and parallel to, the trackbed. **Do not** carry

BROCKHOLLANDS
14
Tufts Farm
The Scowles
Breams Grove
B4234
15
Chel-fridge 13
B4231
The Scowles
Lower Old Bargains Wood
5
To LYDNEY

exhausted near the surface." (These caves, which have been created as a result of the extensive mining owe their origin to the predecessors of that peculiar order of operatives known as the Free Miners of the Forest of Dean.) They have the appearance of either spacious caves, as above Lydney, or of deep stone quarries as at Scowles. Scowles is probably a corruption of the old British word 'crowll' meaning "cave".

on across the line taking the path over the River Lye – the path follows the line for 500m. Although the trackbed extends from Parkend to Lydney Junction, at present passenger services only run from Lydney Junction to Norchard, about a kilometre further south than where you will walk. Even so, the track is occasionally used this far north – so take care to keep a lookout for trains. Trains run between April and December, with a mixture of steam and diesel locomotives.

The Forest of Dean has an area of over 115,000 hectares (according to the Ordnance Survey) and was exploited for its rich minerals from Roman times. The forest has some of the finest woodland scenery to be found anywhere in Britain and has been Crown property since 1016 (although cared for since the 1920s by the Forestry Commission). In

On both sides of the track are great gouges, with the dark red rock sculptured in a great open wound of the landscape. Keep on the track to the B4231 road where, almost opposite, is an unmarked path into Bream's Grove

medieval days it was the main iron working centre of Britain. It is not surprising that railways were built into the forest to exploit this rich mineral supply. Horse tramways were built from 1809, and a canal followed from Lydney to the Severn.

Bradshaw's Manual of 1853 stated: *"The present line for conveying produce of Forest of Dean to Lydney harbour is a descend-*

16

ing line throughout used exclusively for minerals; gradients such as to give impetus to loaded carriages, and to take back empty carriages, 1 in 40 steepest". The tramroad was converted to steam locomotive and rail lines starting in April 1869 (broad gauge!), and rails were re-gauged to standard track in 1872. The track became quite extensive over the next few years as can be seen from the map of forest railways. In its heyday Lydney port had up to 300 small sailing ships in the port waiting to take coal to places like Ilfracombe, the Scilly Isles and Bristol. You will also see that a rail bridge was built over the Severn from Sharpness to the main line at Lydney – the line is now closed and the bridge has been demolished.

To continue with the walk, having walked the line for about 500m you come to the remains of an old bridge abutment (on the left side only). Turn off left after a few metres more and cross the River Lye, noting the old tramway bridge just up river. Pass 'The Homestead' house and onto the B4234 road. Cross and take a track to the left of the electricity distribution station. There is now a long ascent – ignore the track off to left and carry on and then right over a footbridge.

Soilwell

Immediately take the track on the left and then onto a road. Turn left for some 400 metres, and then left into Grove Lane. Just past Grove House, and opposite Woodlands, is a short tarmac track and path going right. Cross scrubland to reach the left side of a sawmill at Soilwell – this name seems to be derived from old English meaning "The muddy wallowing place of a wild boar" or "A pool used as a refuge by a hunted animal".

Pick your way through the piles of sawn logs and through some forlorn Birch trees to a road (Yorkley Lane). Cross the lane and onto a farm track to Soilwell House on the left and Soilwell Cottage on the right, and just past these turn right into a field. Go to the right corner of the field, over a gate and turn right for 20 metres to a lane. Turn left and follow the lane to Oldcroft. Here, turn left at Oldcroft Road, then right onto Church Walk for the walk to meet the 'main' road (from Yorkley to Nibley Green). Turn right and into Viney Hill village.

The village has some very nice houses, with accommodation and a pub.

GR SO 658 066

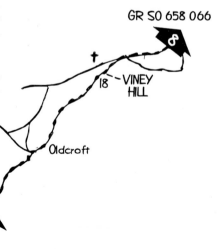

18 VINEY HILL

Oldcroft

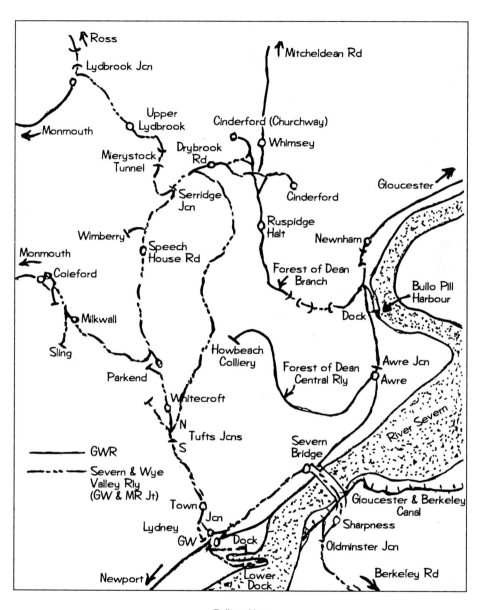

Railway Map

TWO
Viney Hill - Newent
(18.25 miles or 29.2 km)

From the inn continue east on the road until it bends to the right. There are excellent views of the Severn estuary from this point. Leave the main road here and take the unmetalled road going off downhill to the left. This road bends left, then right (ignore a left fork), and finally ends abruptly at a private house gate. Take the footpath to the left of the house and continue downhill (again ignoring a left and a right path off), and arrive at the bottom of the hill and onto an unclassified road. Turn left for 30 metres to a footpath on the right and follow the left fence across a field down to Nibley Mill Farm. The field seems to be a haven for the Cowslip, all too rarely seen these days. Past the farm you reach the A48 road. Turn left, and cross Park End Road.

Should you wish to take a diversion at this stage then Blakeney village is only half a kilometre up the A48 road. To continue the walk take the footpath in the corner of the road, over a footbridge and go half-left, over a stile and up the old railway embankment (this was one of the many lines into the forest and was the Forest of Dean Central Railway from Awre Junction to Howbeach Colliery). On the far embankment side go through a fence 25 metres left of the barn and aim for a stile at the base of the electricity pole at the far side of the field. Once over this stile there is another on your left – ignore it and carry on a straight line behind the house gardens.

When you reach a road, turn left. After some 250 metres you reach Blakeney Hill Road on your left. Carry on the main road past this point. Way ahead can be seen Pylon Hill complete with pylon on top – you are heading for the valley to its right side. Pass a barn on

each side of the road, followed by a footpath on the right. Carry walking on the road verge until you reach Hewlers Farm on the right (which fortunately has a sign to advise you of the farm's name!). Immediately past the farm you will see two footpaths on the left. On the right of the road is a stone slab – go over this slab, alongside the farm, and head for a foot-bridge over Forge Brook at the field bottom. Over the bridge turn left alongside the brook and continue in this direction, over a number of stiles, to follow the beautiful valley. When a gate is reached the buildings of Rowmedley Farm can be seen 150 metres ahead – don't head direct for the farm, but turn right on the other side of the gate and aim for a gap in the far tree line approximately 50 metres from the right hedge. Cross the next field on the same line and go over stile onto a lane.

Turn left on the lane to pass 'The Old Inn', now a private house, and cross Forge Brook. The second gate on the right has a stile. Turn right over this and cross the fields with a fence to your right. Haiebrook Farm comes into view on the far brook side. There is a lot of Common Mouse-ear (*Cerastium fontanum*) growing in these meadows. One more stile brings you to a field with two old barns and Haie Grove Wood starts on the right. Continue on this side of the fence and on this side of the brook – don't go down into the wood! After following the wood to the right for half a kilometre you reach a wood ahead with an inviting stile in the corner. This leads to Newnham and is *not* the GEW. The GEW turns *left* at this point, still within the field, to climb the contours until you reach another wood in front. Carry on the same line over a stile to enter Glastonbury Wood. Turn right almost immediately onto a broad track. This is initially a Scots Pine plantation. Another interesting (if you are that way inclined) piece of information is that we have only three native conifers in the United Kingdom – Scots Pine, Juniper and Yew.

Turn right on the broad forest track and glimpse the River Severn double bend over to the east. The wood changes to Larch trees, and if you are very lucky you may see the Long-eared Owl in this area. There is a two kilometre walk on the broad track through open forest. A number of coloured markers are passed along the route showing laid out forest walks going off the track. The Forest of Dean is now far from wild since the forest is now managed with Spruce, Larch and Fir trees taking over from the Birch, Oak and Ash. You should see the Grey Squirrel and hear the Woodpecker. There are also Deer in the forest.

The Court of Verderers still meets at Speech House. The Court was set up in the 11th century by King Canute to be responsible for anything that grew or lived in the forest. In centuries past the only people found in the forest were there for its natural resources of coal, iron and timber. Timber was supplied for shipbuilding, so vital to British naval power. In Victorian

days the forest produced over a million tons of coal each year.

The forest has a link with Berwick-upon-Tweed, the northern end of the GEW! In 1296 Berwick was under siege and Edward I sent Dean miners to tunnel under the Berwick city walls. As a reward miners were allowed to exploit the forest, and there are still 'Free Miners' with permission to do just that to this day.

To the west of this area of forest lies Lower Soudley which has a heritage centre set beside a mill pond in a valley. The centre tells the fascinating story of the area and has craft shops and a cafe, well worth a visit if you can spare the time. Even further west are the Clearwell caves, ancient iron mines with nine caverns open to the public. There is plenty to occupy you if you wish to linger for a while in the area.

The long forest walk brings you to Blaize Bailey, with a signposted viewpoint just a few metres off the route. Follow the signposts to obtain an expansive view over the river and beyond. There are stone seats to tempt you to stay longer, but return eventually to the forest track. The track soon reaches a forest crossroad. Take the track to the right to a farm and go past to a metalled road and a few houses. Turn left (with more views of the Severn). Just past the last house on the right take a footpath into a field to the right and then walk parallel to the road for 500m before going over a stile back onto the road at Dean Hill. This is now the last view of the River

9

Gill
Glastonbury Birch
Wood   Birch Wood
Wood

Hale
Grove
Wood

21

Halebrook
Farm

Rowmedley
Farm

Forge
Brook

20

Hewter
Farm

GR SO 658 066

19

Disused
Railway

VINEY
HILL

NIBLEY   A48

Severn you will get before you meet up with it again in Shrewsbury city. There is a spectacular view of the great 16km (10 miles) horseshoe bend of the Severn, almost encircling the low lying farmland around Arlingham. The little town of Newnham can be seen at the centre of the loop with its cliff top church. On the other side of the Severn is the old Passage Inn (a solitary building) from which a ferry used to cross to Newnham. To the north-east can be seen the church spire at Westbury-on-Severn. Gloucester Cathedral can also be seen about 17km north-east, with the escarpment of the Cotswold Hills beyond.

There is a crossroad of lanes at Dean Hill. Turn left on a lane for 150 metres to reach a house on the right. Just past this go through a gate to the right and straight downhill over two stiles to emerge on the Littledean Road. Turn left on the road (Silver Street) to walk down to Littledean.

If you turn right at this point for 50 metres you come to the entrance to Little Dean Hall. The hall is open to the public, and is steeped in history – it is claimed that this is the oldest house in England. We suppose that depends on what you mean by a house! As with all old houses, the hall has been built and much altered over many centuries. There is a victorian north front, replacing an earlier georgian one, which in turn replaced a jacobean front. There are remains of a roman building under the walls. The hall has a fine interior and gardens making it a must to visit. The hall is also renowned as one of Britain's most haunted houses.

Having arrived at Littledean town at the bottom of the hill turn left at the mini roundabout onto Broad Street.

Map labels:

DEAN HILL · 10
Wallsprings Wood
Blaize Bailey viewpoint and wood · 23
Dry Wood
Foundry Wood
Dean Heritage Centre · 22
Gill Birch Wood
9

11 · Flaxley Wood
27 · Welshbury Wood Fort
Green Bottom · 26
TIBBSCROSS
Chestnut Inclosure Wood
25
LITTLEDEAN
Littledean Hall
24 · DEAN HILL

Littledean Hall

200m on the right, between the Spar shop and Post Office (and opposite the road to Soudley), is a little lane. Go along the lane to reach a housing estate. Follow the road to the left, then turn right onto Roman Way. When this road turns right there is a gate ahead. Go through the gate and follow the left hedge initially, then bear right to a gate ahead. (The houses at the east side of Cinderford town can be seen on the hill to the west. The name Cinderford means "ford made of cinders", probably made of slag from iron smelting. The ford carried a roman road across Soudley Brook.) Cross the next field to the far right-hand corner. Go through the gate, then cross another field with the hedge to the right. Another gate takes you on the same line (but slightly right) downhill to a footbridge and stile onto a road.

As you enter the road the metalling ends. Turn left. A track takes you into the wood's edge of heavily wooded Chestnuts Hill on

your right. Half a kilometre brings you to a wider track at a T-junction, with a house on the right. Turn right on the new track. Yet another track joins from the right, but keep going left. The houses of Green Bottom hamlet can now be seen down in the valley. The track comes to a gate and stile, and then a few metres later another gate and stile leading to a track.

You now have a choice. You need to turn left here, but a track opposite leads up to the ancient British hill fort of Welshbury at the top of the hill. Precious little can be seen of the fort – you have to imagine earth banks and ditches under the expanse of trees. Its only grace is a distant view of the River Severn at one point. Having visited the fort return down to the track, and turn right (or left if you have not visited the fort). The track traverses round Welshbury Wood. Suddenly the wide forest track ends and you turn right onto a much smaller track with a gradual descent to a minor road that runs from Flaxley to Mitcheldean.

Turn right on the road. The hedgerows are very prolific with wild flowers. There are two slight right bends, then you come to a more pronounced right bend. On the left is a cattle grid and a drive to a house. Go through a gate to the left of the cattle grid, and on a track over a bridge over Westbury Brook. Turn half-left, cross a field and small stream, then bear right and aim for a point in the fence about 50 metres to the left of the stream to find a difficult stile over the fence and onto a forest road. Turn right on the road for about 20 metres, then left on the first of two tracks. Climb rapidly up the contours rising into Flaxley Wood on a little used track. The trees

quite overshadow the path here, but thank goodness that Flaxley and Hope Woods are the last to be encountered for some time! The path is clear as you plod on, and there is some relief with Red Deadnettle (deadnettles do not sting, unlike their cousin the Stinging Nettle), Opposite Leaved Golden Saxifrage, Dog Violet and Bugle to add a little (very little) colour to the route. After a long climb a forest road is reached. Turn right for 25 metres to a crossroads of forest tracks – take the one straight ahead. This is now Hope Wood. After a while

the forest road starts to bend and you have a choice –

1. continue on the forest road as it slowly goes downhill, and you finally reach a footpath sign at a track going off left; or

2. find a track going off to the right and a difficult footpath start, to go downhill some 200 metres parallel to the right of the forest track above. The path eventually comes downhill to join the forest track. Turn left for 100 metres, then right at the signpost mentioned in option 1 above.

Either way, go through a gate to emerge at the north end of Hope Wood and into a field.

Take the track down towards the A4136 road. Just before the road turn right in the field, and keep barns and stream on the left. Go through an old apple orchard to find a stile, and keep on this line heading to the south of all buildings, through stiles and gates, until you reach a very large farm barn on your left. There is a bungalow on your right now. Pass to the right of the barn, and just beyond it pass over a stile on the left to continue on the same line – even when the right fence bends away – and head for a distant stile and footbridge. Then, over a further stile, you will see two stiles on your left – take the stile furthest away up to the A4136 road.

Turn right on the road, and over an old railway line (although little sign remains now of the old line from Ross-on-Wye to Gloucester). You shortly reach a war memorial on the left. Turn up the old lane here (and we mean *up* – the lane is about 1 in 2!). Mellick and Betony grow in the hedgerow. Surprisingly, there are a number of houses on this very steep lane. The lane eventually levels out and joins the main A4136 again. Turn left, then immediately left again on a metalled track. (If you wish to carry on the A4136 for

Descending May Hill

another 100 metres you reach a turn leading to Blakemore Farm which is a mohair, silk and craft centre – a working farm with refreshments and Bed & Breakfast).

The metalled track passes a farm on the right. Then, at a dump for old machinery, it changes to a narrow footpath, but is still obvious. You meet signs for paths going to left and right, but ignore them and carry straight on to enter a Gloucestershire Wildlife nature reserve. This is a most beautiful area through woodland with Toothwort (a parasite living on Hazel or Maple) and Wood Spurge. There is an old cliff face on the left. You leave the reserve via a gate onto a wide track. There should now be a stile to the right through the hedge leading to a path running almost parallel to the track. This is blocked in 1996, so

May Hill Signs

until this is cleared walk down the wide track for approx 140 metres and through a gate on the right. Then turn left to follow the hedge line until a bungalow is reached (over a hedge to left). Go through a gate and follow the right fence for a few metres, then another gate (ignoring a left gate) and follow the broken hedge on the left to reach a stile and steps down to the A40 road. Cross the road with care to the road junction and sign for May Hill opposite. This is Dursley Cross.

Walk up the road and take the second turn on the left (Yartleton Lane). After 100 metres turn right on a bridleway (now a metalled road). Pass four houses on the left and a footpath to the right. The metalling then ends and you are on an earth track which leads up to a gate. **Don't** go through the gate, but turn right on the track just before the gate. The path is now in a thin strip of woodland. After 200 metres you meet a road. Turn left for 100 metres to a junction of paths. Turn sharp left up a track to enter the National Trust land of May Hill. Follow the path through Bracken, Rosebay Willowherb and Conifer trees. As you climb, a vista opens up to the southwest and the Severn can be seen in the far distance. Ignore a path to the left and go through a gate onto a wide forest track. Follow the tree line on the right, climbing all the time. When the tree line ends paths split off, but carry on directly ahead heading towards a small conifer plantation on the very top of May Hill. There is a trig point (296 metres), and the remains of an ancient Briton hill embankment. On a clear day you can see the Bristol Channel.

The trees were planted originally by Longhope parish council, and replenished by the May Hill preservation society in 1977 to mark the Queen's silver jubilee. Take the track to the

right of the trees and descend to the NT sign and boundary fence. Through the gate there are now four paths – one goes left along the wall (ignore), one straight ahead (ignore), one going down to the right (follow), and one off into the dense wood to far right (ignore). The correct path now descends through Bracken. There are side turns, but keep on the direct main route dropping downhill to reach a metalled road. Turn right on the road and eventually you meet houses and The Yew Tree Inn and then a road junction. This is Clifford's Mesne. The old name for this place was *Clifford's Meend* in 1749, which means "Okle Clifford's forest waste". The new name is probably better!
Cross the road, and go along path opposite to left of house. You soon reach house gardens to the left as you progress through a small wood. A footbridge brings you to another track, on which you turn left

through a dark tunnel of trees for 50 metres to reach a road. Turn right on the road for 200 metres to a crossroads (with post box and telephone kiosk). Turn left at the village hall and up the wide track opposite. 150 metres brings you to a transverse track. Carry on beyond this for a further 150 metres to a road. Turn right and, when the road turns sharp left, carry straight on a green track. Go under two lines of pylon wires. 150 metres past the second line, and at end of field on left, turn left up a path. Go uphill to a road and a house. Turn left for 30 metres, and then turn right, having passed the house, through a gate into Acorn Wood.

You are now on a clear path in this beautiful natural wood. Pass two paths going off left and carry on the distinct path forward. There are lots of Knapweed, Common Centaury, Silverweed, Broom, Hedge Woundwort,

Wood Sage, Selfheal, Oak and Birch in the wood. Suddenly you come to a point where there is an open field to your right and a wire fence. *Do not* carry on the obvious path forward, but go over the wire fence to the right where there *should* be a stile. Turn left, and walk in the field parallel to the wood (still on your left) to reach a gate. Go through the gate and follow the right hedge to shortly reach a wire fence and an immediate overgrown gate, over which you follow the right hedge for 300 metres to a gate on the right. Go through this gate and follow the left hedge for 100 metres to a stile, go over and turn right along hedge for a few metres to a poultry shed on the right. Turn left along the farm drive from here, and through gates to reach the road. The National Birds of Prey Centre is only 500m south on this road.

Cross the road and enter the market garden of

Newent Market Hall

again and becomes wider. Cross a bridge and arrive at the B4216 road (Culver Street). Turn left to Newent centre.

In the *Domesday Book* the town was called *Noent* meaning "New Place". The river on which the town is based is the Leadon – the area is sometimes referred to as the Vale of Leadon. This area is often called the

GR SO 722 259

forgotten part of Gloucestershire, but the area used to be called Ryelands (from the growing of the Rye cereal) and the Ryeland sheep was the local breed. The town was settled in Roman times and in its time was very important with an iron works and a coal mine. The railway closed many years ago – the line used to run from Gloucester to Ledbury, with about 22 minutes running time from Gloucester and a further 25 minutes to Ledbury – and the canal has also disappeared. The town has an atmosphere of time standing still, with its 17th century market place. It also has a Shambles museum of Victorian life. Further north we come across the birthplaces of famous classical composers, but Newent itself was the birthplace in 1929 of Joe Meek, Britain's first independent pop record producer who made the first recordings of Rod Stewart, Tom Jones and Screaming Lord Sutch. He also composed *Johnny Remember Me* and *Telstar.*

Great Boulsdon Farm. This is a farm where the crop varies in its position from year to year, but a route is signposted through the crops. Go to the right of the greenhouses, then left for 100 metres and then right downhill through the fruit crop. You pass a large pond on the right and go over a stile to walk parallel to a stream.

Follow the path to pass to the right of Brook Farm and onto a road. Turn right for 20 metres, then left via a gate to continue following the stream. The path goes slightly away from the stream, then through a stile and turns right down towards the stream again (don't cross the stream over a footbridge). Continue until you reach houses, where the path turns left and passes a school playing field. The path turns right to bring you to an estate road. Cross the road and go onto a tarmac path leading into the outskirts of Newent. Ignore a left turn and follow the path until it turns right and crosses a cul-de-sac road. The track then meets the stream

THREE
Newent - Great Malvern
(18.5 miles or 29.6 km)

The town of Newent is lucky to have a large lake. The walk continues from Broad Street. Go along the alley opposite the Red Lion Inn and follow the sign for Newent Lake until you reach the end of the lake (public conveniences are in the public car park to the left). Ignore the footpath sign and go to the end of the lake dam, then walk along the lake's right side on the permissive path.

The lake is quite long, and popular with the locals. Having reached the lake's far end turn off right to the children's play area, and the path going right out of this area – which goes parallel to the town's bypass road. You finally reach a public footpath and turn left to the

Newent bypass – note the 'Igloo' energy efficient houses to your right. Cross the busy road to a kissing gate and path opposite. Cross the field, footbridge, kissing gate and another footbridge and then follow the wide path to yet another kissing gate onto a road at Lancaster Terrace. This area is also called Stardens, which was first recorded in 1286 as *Sterdenne* which means "valley below the projecting tongue of land".

Take the road opposite and immediately go off diagonally right alongside the greenhouses. At the rear of these greenhouses is a huge field without any signposts. However, over to the right is Newton farmhouse. Strike out across the field (on a tractor line through the crop if possible) and keep about 150 metres parallel to the left of the farm and on a line to the left of the two electricity poles. Carry on this line right across the field to reach the poultry sheds on their left side (and their smell). With luck you will see a footpath sign at the end of the sheds. Go over a stile and along a narrow fenced path to pass a house, and go over a stile onto a road. Turn left for 100 metres on the road to find a stile on the right, just alongside a garage.

Going over the stile should allow you to cross a field – go through a hedge stile, cross a field and pass over the driveway of Newbarn Farm to reach a hedge on the left which is followed

Stallard Poultry Farm

39

Brand Green

6

Alt Route via road If path blocked

Newbarn Farm

Poultry Sheds

Newton Farm 38

6 Glasshouses

Lancaster Terrace

Lake

37

5 B4216

NEWENT
GR SO 722 259

for 250 metres to meet a gate on the left and a path going off right.*

Unfortunately, in 1996, both the first hedge and the farm drive are blocked. Until these are cleared by Gloucestershire County Council pass the stile going off the road and continue on the road for almost 400 metres to a road junction. Turn right for about 900 metres until you almost reach Stallards poultry farm and pass through a gate on the right to strike out at right angles to the hedge* and cross the field.

The opposite fence line comes from the right, then turns and goes away from you – aim for this point, and carry on the same straight line with the fence now on your right. Cross a stile to bring the fence onto your left, and then a stile into a small rough area. Go right for about 25 metres, then over stile on left into a very large field. Over to the right you can see a long line of trees. The path goes to a point half way up this line through whatever crop is planted. You may prefer to go right, then left around the crop to reach the trees. Whichever way you go climb over a stile into the tree line and carry on the same direction through the thin line to emerge over two more stiles into a field. Head slightly left towards Brand Green hamlet. Go to the left of a paddock and

Payford Mill

4l

Pauntley Court

Pauntley Church

old huts, then take a stile to enter the back garden of a bungalow. Cross the right side of the lawn of the bungalow and go through a gate

40

onto an access track. Turn right for 15 metres then bear left onto a path, as the track bears right, for a further 15 metres. Take the left fork onto a short path to a 'main road'.

Turn right on the road and walk past 'St Oswalds' house, and then to a metal gate on the left. Go through the gate and aim for a gate on the far side of the field, then half-right to find an old metal gate in the next fence. You now face a long field, usually ploughed. Way off to the right is a wood. Between the wood and yourself is a dip going across the field. Head for the furthest away point of the dip (in essence to the right of Pauntley Court which can now be seen in the distance). At the far field side go over a gate and into a field. Follow the right fence and onto a track to Pauntley Court Farm. Walk through the farmyard. The church of St John-the-Evangelist is now reached, with Pauntley Court to its left side. Pauntley means "clearing in the valley".

Pauntley Court was the home of Richard Whittington, the Dick Whittington of legend. There is quite a difference between fact and fiction. The legend says he went to London as a poor boy with his cat because he heard that the streets of London were paved with gold, and only the call of Bow Bells prevented his leaving before making his fortune. There is also an old rhyme —

Turn again Whittington
Thrice mayor of London.

The fact is that Dick's father was Sir William de Whittington, who owned the Court, and whilst they may not have been fabulously rich, they were not penniless. Dick became a merchant trader and did very well for himself, even lending money to both Richard II and Henry IV. He was in fact Lord Mayor of London four times in 1397, 1398, 1406 and 1419. He was born about 1355 and died in 1423.

The church is very beautiful and was built by the Normans about 1170. A Norman nave and chancel arch still remain, and there are numerous remains from the 16th, 17th and 18th centuries. A leaflet is available for a small charge which gives the full details of the church and the story of Dick Whittington.

Pauntley is in the Vale of Leadon, which is an intensive agricultural area as you will have seen from the many arable fields. From the church go to the left of the private buildings of Pauntley Court, through a gate and onto a track. When the track ends cross a stile and go through a field, with the fence on your left, as you head for Payford Bridge. As you near a road turn left through a gate onto the road. Turn right to pass over a bridge alongside the river, and then a bridge proper over the River Leadon at Payford Bridge. A road joins from the left once over the bridge. You should take the footpath to the right at that point, and then immediately turn left uphill in lovely open woodland. At the end of the wood go through a gate into a field. Head straight across the field to a gate onto a metalled minor road. This little used road is often covered with wind blown sand from the fields, and from here you get your first

glimpse of the Malvern Hills to the north.

Cross the road, and go at right angles across the next field – of very fine sand – going slightly left to a right angled turn in the far hedge. A few metres down the left side of the hedge is a gate on the left. Go through and follow the fence now on your right, heading in the direction of the houses at Waysmeet. Keep to the left of the fence all the way, then negotiate two gates to carry on the same line. Aim for the left of the farm and go through the gate to exit onto a road. There is one straight through road and a T-junction road, together with four footpaths meeting here. 'Waysmeet' is a very apt name for the hamlet.

Turn right on the road for 50 metres to two gates on the left. Go through the second gate and head at right angles away from the road, keeping to the right side of the hedge at the end of the first field. Go over a stile and head slightly right to clear a kink in the next hedgerow, but still keep on the same line – over stiles and a footbridge – until you enter a field with a hedge to the right. Plod on in a generally northerly direction – the hills ahead are getting slowly closer. One transverse path is crossed, and eventually you

EGGS TUMP
18
M50
Bury Court
Park Farm
44
Hanover Court
Pool
Alt Road Route
A417
43
REDMARLEY D'ABITOT
42
WAYSMEET
Payford Bridge
17

Pauntley Court

cross a stile to put the hedge to your left (ignore a path going off to the left). You now find yourself in the cricket field of Redmarley D'Abitot Cricket Club. Go down the left side of the field to pass the pavilion. Take care of any 4's or 6's during play, and get onto the track at the far field side to lead onto the road at Redmarley. The Post Office and village store is 25 metres to your right, with the inn some 300 metres beyond that.

The intriguing village name means "The clearing near the reedy pool". D'Abitot was the name of the feudal owner, Urse D'Abitot.

The next 1.7km going north has some very bad paths at present (1996). The map shows some very well positioned paths but, until the county council carry out the remedial work necessary to make the paths walkable, you have a choice —

1. having arrived at the road, after leaving the cricket pitch, turn right to the Post Office. Just before it turn left on a minor road which leads to the A417 after 300 metres. Turn left on the busy A417 for 750 metres, then right onto a minor road (leading to the B4208) for 400 metres to reach Bury Court.

or

2. you may be lucky and find that the paths have been put into good order by the time you are walking the route, in which case —

Having arrived at the road, after leaving the cricket pitch, turn left for 200 metres until just past the last house on the right where a stile should take you into a field. After 50 metres go over a stile to the left to the far left field corner, through a stile, and then follow right hedge to emerge onto a very narrow lane. Turn left for 200 metres to find a footpath sign(!) and cross a field with a wooden fence to your right. At the field end **don't** go through a gate, but climb over the fence to its right and cross the next field on its left side with a pond to your left in a dip. Keep the hedge to the left, and at the end of the field you come to the back garden fence of a house. The path is blocked here, but should go through the garden to an access road. Once on this access road you will see a stile in the field corner opposite, enabling you to cross the field and go over a stile onto the main A417 road. You should then cross the road direct, and go through a gate, to follow the left broken hedge to a footbridge over a stream. The bridge is there, but in 1996 was badly in need of attention. From this bridge you should then climb the field to the left of a fence – this is heavily barbed off at present. The path arrives at a gate onto a farm track from Park Farm. Turn left on the track to reach the road at Bury Court.

Unfortunately in 1996 the first alternative is the only one walkable – unless Gloucestershire County Council have put the paths into order!

Whichever way you have arrived at the road at Bury Court – carry on northeast on the road. Shortly cross the M50 motorway, a busy road, but nowhere near as busy or noisy as the M6 to come in Cheshire!

There is now a 2.4km (1.5miles) road walk, which will come as something of a welcome relief if you have fought your way through the alternative 2 from Redmarley, but the road is very quiet and little used. After the motorway walk on the road to pass a turn off to the right and reach a junction off to the left. Turn left here to the hamlet of Eggs Tump (where do these names come from?) where the road bears right. Follow this road until another joins from the left. Turn right along this combined road until you come to a road junction off to the right. Go past this junction for some

Conservators Sign

200 metres until you come to a farm on the right (Gate House) and a barn to the left. Turn off onto a footpath just before the barn, and go up the field with a stone wall to the left, to reach a gate into a wood at the southern end of Chase End Hill. This is the start of the long ridge walk of the Malvern Hills. The Malvern Hills were probably formed by volcanic action some 300 million years ago, although the rock which was forced upwards is said to be about 600 million years old. The name Malvern is of Celtic origin – *moel* and *bryn* meaning "bald hill".

The counties of Hereford and Worcester are now administered jointly, but the county boundary of the once two separate counties runs largely on the ridge of the Malvern Hills. Although it has disappeared in parts, much of the medieval *Shire Ditch* can still be seen. The ditch was built by Gilbert de Clare, the Earl of Gloucester, to separate his land from that of the Bishop of Hereford. It was constructed between 1287 and 1291.

Having entered the wood at the southern end of the hill, cross a track and carry on uphill. As a track goes off to the left, turn right uphill for a short distance and then carry straight on over a transverse track. Then begin the climb up Chase End Hill to reach the triangulation point at 191 metres (it sounded much better when it was 627 feet). You now begin to appreciate that even though the summits may be low in height by comparison to some of the Pennine peaks, the walk over the ridge is still quite a stiff walk. Ragged Stone Hill is now looking very inviting to the north, but from here not much can be seen of the ridge further north.

From the trig point turn left, and downhill, to the path which can just be made out below heading to the houses of Whiteleaved Oak. Reach a clear path at the hill base and follow this to the minor road. Near to the post box is the boundary of the three counties of

Herefordshire, Worcestershire and Gloucestershire. There is no sign of an Oak tree with white leaves here now, which originally gave its name to the hamlet! Turn right on the road and follow it round to the right, past houses on the left, until you reach a track going off diagonally on the left. Go through a gate and up the track. Soon, a path joins from the right and you have two left forks – a path straight uphill and a fairly wide level track. Take the uphill path on the left and continue climbing until you reach the top of Ragged Stone Hill at 254 metres. The

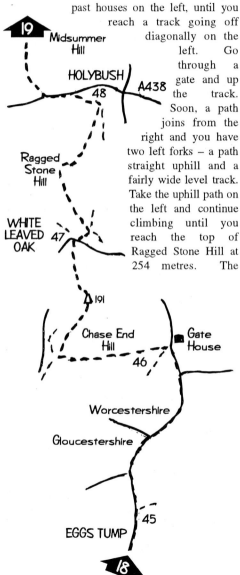

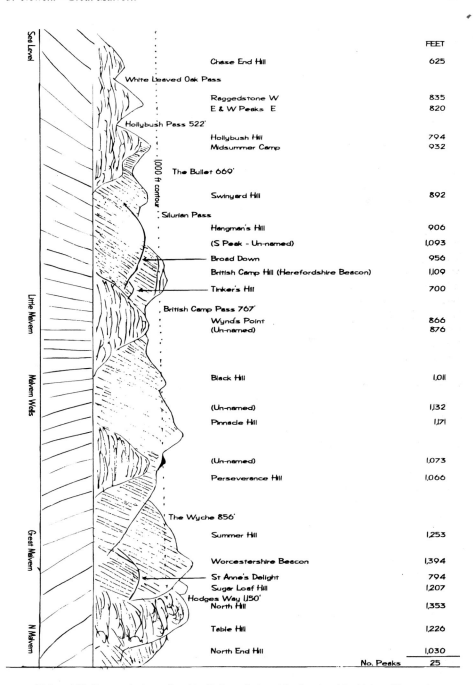

	FEET
Chase End Hill	625
White Leaved Oak Pass	
Raggedstone W	835
E & W Peaks E	820
Hollybush Pass 522'	
Hollybush Hill	794
Midsummer Camp	932
1,000 ft contour	
The Bullet 669'	
Swinyard Hill	892
Silurian Pass	
Hangman's Hill	906
(S Peak - Un-named)	1,093
Broad Down	956
British Camp Hill (Herefordshire Beacon)	1,109
Tinker's Hill	700
British Camp Pass 767'	
Wynd's Point	866
(Un-named)	876
Black Hill	1,011
(Un-named)	1,132
Pinnacle Hill	1,171
(Un-named)	1,073
Perseverance Hill	1,066
The Wyche 856'	
Summer Hill	1,253
Worcestershire Beacon	1,394
St Anne's Delight	794
Sugar Loaf Hill	1,207
Hodges Way 1,150'	
North Hill	1,353
Table Hill	1,226
North End Hill	1,030
No. Peaks	25

Sea Level · Little Malvern · Malvern Wells · Great Malvern · N Malvern

Malvern Hills Topography (reproduced by kind permission of the Curator of the Malvern Museum)

views are now more extensive at this greater height than those from Chase End. There is another 'peak' to your right which looks as if it just might be taller, but no it isn't – it's 250 metres! Make your way to this second peak, then turn north (left) and head for the right side of the wood in front. This is Winter Coombe Wood and is owned by the National Trust. Go straight down the right side of the wood to meet a vehicle track near the bottom. Turn left on the track to the A438 road at Hollybush. There is a local story that a monk from Little Malvern Priory had to crawl, on his hands and knees, to the top of Ragged Stone Hill to do penance.

Turn left on the road. After 100 metres cross from Worcestershire into Herefordshire. The large Hollybush sandstone quarry is on the right of the road. The road climbs up to go through the 'pass' of the hills. As you reach the top of the climb there is a large car/coach park on the right with a wide track to its left. Cross the road and go onto this track. There is a signpost here telling you that you are now on the Worcestershire Way, a 'short' long distance path going north more or less on the same route as the GEW.

Follow the metalled private road, which soon changes to an earth vehicle track. Eastnor Castle can just be made out to the west and is about 2.5km distant. The castle is a 'modern' building, having only been built in 1812 (what must have been in the builders minds at that time? This was the year of the great reversal of fortune for Napoleon, with his retreat from Moscow). The castle was built for Lord Somers – the architect was Robert Smirke (who went on to design the British museum). Extensive alterations were carried out later in the 19th century by Pugin. The castle is now the home of the Hervey-Bathurst family. There is an arboretum and lake, and the interior is quite splendid. The castle is open to the public, normally from Easter to the end of September on Sundays,

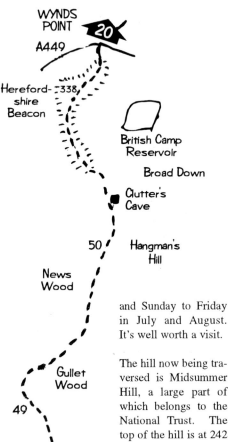

and Sunday to Friday in July and August. It's well worth a visit.

The hill now being traversed is Midsummer Hill, a large part of which belongs to the National Trust. The top of the hill is at 242 metres and has a large ancient Briton hill fort, built about 400BC. The fort is smaller than the one on Herefordshire Beacon ahead, and is bypassed.

The obelisk of Eastnor Castle is now very clear on the unnamed hill to the north west. The structure was erected by Lord Somers in 1812 in memory of his son who was killed in that year in the siege of Burgos (in Spain) in the Peninsula War. The track climbs slowly and you pass Castle Copse cottage on your left. The cottage has an interesting topography print fastened to its garage wall which shows all the peaks of the Malvern hills as seen from the east. Carry on the track and you reach a vehicle track going off right to Midsummer Cottage. The track ahead bears left and down to woodland. As you reach the bottom there is a track going off, and down, to the right to the Gullet through a natural pass in the hills. A track goes off left and climbs to the obelisk, should you wish to visit.

To continue on the GEW carry on the track through woodland as you walk northeastwards with News Wood to the left and Gullet Wood to the right. Eventually you reach open land with a junction of tracks. Turn right to reach the top of Swinyard Hill and the *Shire Ditch*.

You will now keep the ditch company for most of its route northwards. Turn left on the hilltop and walk along the ditch. After half a kilometre the track picks up other paths, but bear right and keep below the top of Hangman's Hill where criminals were once hanged. Keep below the ditch, with News Wood down to your left. Keep on this line as the higher land of Broad Down is to the right. The very large British Camp is now ahead (and this is a very extensive fort site). Keeping below the ditch line brings you to a small rock outcrop, and in the rock is Clutter's Cave. The cave is man-made, but who Clutter was isn't known. The probability is that Clutter was a hermit who made the cave in medieval times. Should the weather be inclement this makes a good shelter until the rain abates! Legend has it that the Welsh prince Owain Glyndwr hid here after losing a battle against the English on Herefordshire Beacon in 1405.

Past the cave follow the contour to a coll and a stone marker, then turn half-left to climb the stone anti-erosion steps up to the British camp. You are now at 338 metres. The camp

Part of the Malvern Hills

was obviously very large, occupying some 13 hectares, and dates from about the 3rd century BC. Remains of the earth embankments are still very clear. Some of the flat areas near the fort had Iron Age dwellings, which probably disappeared as the Romans invaded. British Camp Reservoir, built in 1892, is down to the east and the outskirts of Little Malvern can be seen to the northeast.

There are a number of publications available should you wish to learn more about the Malvern hill forts or what life was like living on the hilltops in those troubled times.

The name of Sir Edward Elgar (who was born in Broadheath in 1857) will be forever associated with the Malvern area, and we are indebted to C J Bennett of The Elgar Foundation for the following information —

"Elgar was always inspired by his surroundings and of course the Malvern Hills played a central role in his life. He lived in and around the Hills – in several different houses – for almost fifteen years (1891-1904), and he probably knew the hills and surrounding area like the back of his hand. He liked nothing better than being in the open air, going for long walks and cycle rides; kite flying on the Hills or fishing on the Severn, Teme or Wye; always taking notebooks with him and jotting down any musical ideas that might come to him.

You could argue that most of Elgar's music was, in one way or another,

inspired by the Hills, but it is hard to connect particular pieces to specific places; although his cantata "Caractacus" of 1898 is closely linked with Herefordshire Beacon (British Camp). In Victorian times it was thought that Caractacus's defence against the advancing Roman army was centred on this hill fort, and the cantata is based on this legend. It is now known that Caractacus' fort was elsewhere, though of course Elgar did not know this".

Elgar, who was mainly self taught, was living in Malvern Wells when he composed, amongst other works, the first two *Pomp and Circumstance* marches – *Cockaigne* and *The Apostles*. He wrote the ode *Land of Hope and Glory*, set to his *Pomp and Circumstance* march for the coronation of Edward VII in August 1902. He was knighted in 1904 and awarded the Order of Merit in 1911. He was also the conductor with the Three Choirs Festival. Elgar's name will arise again on the walk.

The Herefordshire Beacon, to give the point its proper name, is a good place to linger. To continue, walk down the stone and metalled track to the car park and Wynds Point where the A449 road comes past to join Ross-on-Wye to Malvern.

A detour to Little Malvern will enable you to see the remains of the 12th century Little Malvern Benedictine Priory if you have the time. Sir Edward Elgar died in 1934 and he, and his family, are buried in St Wulstan's churchyard.

Cross over onto the B4232 road going north, then just past the public conveniences (on the left) take the footpath going off diagonally to the right and immediately fork to the right to go up onto a terrace area with seats. Pass the seats and turn left (north), onto the *Shire Ditch*. There are numerous paths going north to Wyche Cutting, but most walkers take the ditch path along the hill tops. There are no outstanding peaks, more a series of small hills – the highest point being called Pinnacle Hill (357 metres) – but you do see Little Malvern and Malvern Wells down to the right, along with the large Three Counties showground which hosts several agricultural shows each year. You pass over the railway tunnel, bored through the heart of the hill far below. Ignore all joining paths and keep going north, and up and down all the hillocks. There are a number of very nice seats provided along the route if you require 'five minutes' rest before continuing. You finally reach some steps leading down to the B4218 road at the Wyche Cutting – the name comes from old English meaning "a salt cutting". The packhorses would have brought salt to Malvern this way. There are toilets here, a tea shop to the left and shops to the right.

Opposite the toilets take the middle road (Beacon Road) for 100 metres. Turn off after the last house on a diagonal path going right. The path bears right, then left onto the *Shire Ditch* ridge. There is Bracken and Gorse as you walk along. From the top of the ridge there are extensive views to both west and east. You soon arrive at a stone topography and a tarmac drive. Leave the tarmac and walk on the *Shire Ditch* to its right. Upper Wyche covered reservoir is to the right (Severn Trent Water). There is a slight summit before the dip of Firs Valley, and then you go on and off the tarmac drive again before taking the earth track directly up to the summit of Worcestershire Beacon. This is the highest point of the Malvern Hill range at 425 metres (1,395 feet). Just beyond the trig point is a stone view point erected to commemorate Queen Victoria's 60th jubilee in 1897.

The views are extensive since this is the highest point for many miles. To the southwest is Ledbury and the Woolhope Hills, with Mynydd Maen way off in the distance; to the west is Hereford and Radnor Forest; northwest is Cleobury Mortimer and the Clee Hills; northeast you can see to Birmingham and the Lickey Hills; to the east is Pershore, Broadway and Arbury Hill; southeast are the Cotteswold Hills (note the old spelling); to the south is Bath; and to the south south west are the Mendip Hills and the Bristol Channel. On a very clear day the Wrekin can be seen to the north some 60km away. You can also see the three great Cathedrals of Gloucester, Hereford and Worcester (which holds the tomb of the infamous King John). The site has been used for warning beacons for well over 400 years, and it is said that when a beacon was lit to warn of the approach of the Spanish Armada it was seen from 12 counties. Edward VII

GR SO 775 459

St Ann's Well

O Viewpoint

55

GREAT MALVERN

22

425 Worcestershire Beacon

54 Firs Valley

B4232

B4218

21

Worcestershire Beacon

visited the top – he was driven up most of the way!

From the beacon take the path directly down to the dip of Green Valley and another stone viewpoint. At this point turn right (east) to descend a clear path for about 150 metres, then take a hairpin turn left down to join a broad track – *note this point for the next stage*. Turn right on the track which runs above Green Valley down to your left. Turn right again at a junction to reach St Ann's Well.

This place is thought to have been inhabited well before the 13th century. St Ann was a medieval patroness of wells and springs. The purity of the water began to attract large numbers of visitors from the 18th century. This is real Malvern water, and it is free to drink!

There is a plaque on the building —

In memory of George Pullen
"Blind George"
who for over 50 years played
his harmonium at St Ann's well
Died Feb 23rd 1936

Malvern water today is bottled by the Schweppes company on the other side of the hill at Colwall.

From here it is straightforward and downhill all the way – first on a hairpin drive then right on a tarmac drive, and finally steps down to Great Malvern.

The town has a number of attractions. The Malvern museum should perhaps be the first port of call. The museum is housed in one of the two buildings surviving from the Benedictine monastery (the other being Malvern Priory church). The building dates from 14th century and has a number of rooms to visit, namely the Geological, Medieval,

Water Cure, Victorian, Modern and Staircase Gallery. The museum is open daily in season with a small entrance fee.

The town is famous for its private schools, and also as the birthplace of the Morgan car.

A visit to Malvern Priory is essential. There are so many things to see in the priory that a description would not do justice. Suffice to repeat a report from Nehemiah Wharton, one of Cromwell's men in 1642, on Great Malvern Priory church: *"Statlyest parrish church in England, adorned with varieties of rarities"*.

There is a shop in the priory which you should see before you end your visit.

St Ann's Well

FOUR
Great Malvern - Great Witley
(20 miles or 32 km)

There are many attractions in Great Malvern, but you must continue the walk. Retrace your steps back up the hill to St Ann's well and the broad track beyond. However, when you reach the point where you joined this broad track don't deviate, but carry on the track to meet a wide transverse track. Cross this and your track changes from stony to short grass, with a stone marker signed "Sugarloaf". You soon reach the very top of the valley with extensive views. Turn right towards the point between Table Hill to the left and North Hill to the right (with End Hill peeping between) but only go for 50 metres, before turning left to go round the west flank of Table Hill.

St Ann's Well

There are good views down to West Malvern from this path. As you reach the west side of Table Hill you meet a transverse track. Turn left along this for 20 metres before turning off right, back on yourself but on a lower track. After 150 metres the track forks. Take the left fork. The path gradually descends until houses can be seen through trees to your left. A path joins from the left and the house gardens become closer. The track now splits into two broad tracks. Take the right fork uphill. This track has been cobbled at some historical time (from the North Malvern quarries?). From this point Clee Hill is some 35km to the northwest. The track turns sharp right and then sharp left as you descend rapidly through woods to join the B4232 road.

Turn left on the road for 50 metres, then right onto a path which takes 95 steps down to a minor road. Turn right on this road (ignore the beckoning stile ahead into a field) for 100 metres, then left over a stile and into an enclosed way for a path and 29 steps down to the B4219 road (there is a drinking fountain on your left here: *"Presented by William Earl Beauchamp in 1905 to the people of Cowleigh"*).

Turn left for 100 metres to take the third drive off to the right. There is a noticeboard here with information on the Worcestershire Way which runs with the GEW for the next 2.5km. Perhaps there will be something similar for the GEW one day!

Follow the wide farm drive to reach a tree line. Continue on the drive through the trees and onto the path on the right just inside the trees to emerge in a field. Follow the tree line on your right and keep going until the trees end and you go over a stile. Turn left and over a footbridge, then turn right to follow the hedge line for 100 metres before leaving it diagonally left for a short time and rejoining it again at a stile. Now follow the broad track through an Apple orchard. At the far side turn left for 30 metres, then go over a footbridge on the right. Bear half-right after 20 metres to follow the track through another orchard and reach the left side of a wood. Cross a stile and follow the left wood side until it ends and you continue with a hedge to the right. You arrive at a minor road, which is crossed, and the path opposite taken which goes on the right side of a field and over a gate onto a drive leading to the A4103 road. The New Inn is opposite.

Cross the road and go to the left side of the field as you climb and emerge onto an earth road. The Worcestershire Way leaves here, but you should turn right along the road for 200 metres to meet a tarmac road. Turn left on the tarmac road (marked "private" to keep out cars, but public for walkers). After 600 metres you arrive at The Norrest with its pool and large lake – a farm now with outbuildings converted to private housing.

Not far to the west is Birchwood Lodge, where Sir Edward Elgar once lived. We are again indebted to C J Bennett of the Elgar Foundation for the following —

"Birchwood Lodge is a rather plain house, but in a beautiful position just north of the hills where much of the "Dream of Gerontius" was composed. This house was a particular favourite of Elgar's, and it broke his heart when he realised that the lease could not be renewed and he would have to leave." By 1902 the piece was acclaimed as a masterpiece by Richard Strauss who said: *"With that work England became for the first time one of the modern states".*

meeting with other clerics.

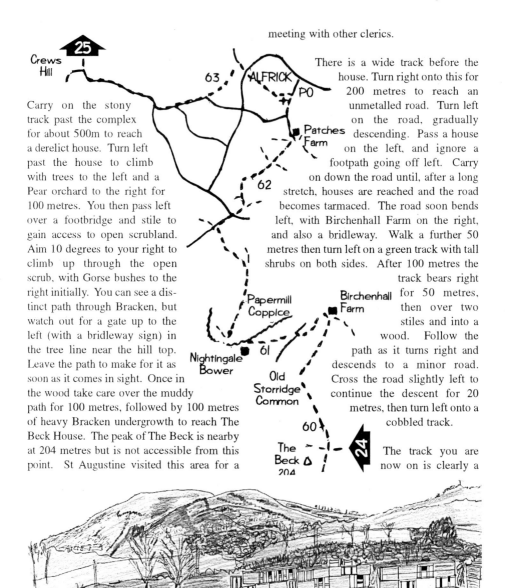

There is a wide track before the house. Turn right onto this for 200 metres to reach an unmetalled road. Turn left on the road, gradually descending. Pass a house on the left, and ignore a footpath going off left. Carry on down the road until, after a long stretch, houses are reached and the road becomes tarmaced. The road soon bends left, with Birchenhall Farm on the right, and also a bridleway. Walk a further 50 metres then turn left on a green track with tall shrubs on both sides. After 100 metres the track bears right for 50 metres, then over two stiles and into a wood. Follow the path as it turns right and descends to a minor road. Cross the road slightly left to continue the descent for 20 metres, then turn left onto a cobbled track.

Carry on the stony track past the complex for about 500m to reach a derelict house. Turn left past the house to climb with trees to the left and a Pear orchard to the right for 100 metres. You then pass left over a footbridge and stile to gain access to open scrubland. Aim 10 degrees to your right to climb up through the open scrub, with Gorse bushes to the right initially. You can see a distinct path through Bracken, but watch out for a gate up to the left (with a bridleway sign) in the tree line near the hill top. Leave the path to make for it as soon as it comes in sight. Once in the wood take care over the muddy path for 100 metres, followed by 100 metres of heavy Bracken undergrowth to reach The Beck House. The peak of The Beck is nearby at 204 metres but is not accessible from this point. St Augustine visited this area for a

The track you are now on is clearly a

North Hill from The Norrest

very old lane which was not adopted when cars took over from horses and carts. Follow the track as it goes downhill through thick woodland, with the sunlight filtering through fitfully, until you arrive at Nightingale Bower house. The track ends here, and you cross the footbridge over Leigh Brook.

26

River Teme

Ankerdine Farm

66
Inn

KNIGHTWICK

A44

Knightwick Bridge
River Teme

✝ Knightwick Church

Lord's
65 Wood

Coal
Pits
Wood

Disused
Railway

Round
Hill
64

Crews
Hill **25**

The far bank gives access to The Knapp and Papermill Nature Reserve, managed by the Worcestershire Nature Conservation Trust. This area has many Butterfly species, and also Snakes – you should hear Grasshoppers in summer.

From the footbridge turn left for 10 metres, then go diagonally right up the bank and through a kissing gate into a field. Head half-right across the field and up a

very wide green track between woods at the far end to gain access to another smaller field. Find the stile in the far left corner and enter Papermill Coppice Wood. 100 metres brings you to a transverse track (with a signpost pointing right). Take the track to the LEFT towards the left wood edge for 200 metres to reach a T-junction. Turn left for 20 metres until the track turns right and becomes much broader. Follow the track (ignoring the path off to right) which becomes an old green lane taking you to a house drive. Turn left on the drive to reach a road at Alfrick Pound.

Turn right for 200 metres to a road junction. 10 metres further turn left on a path and over a stile. Turn right in the field alongside the right hedge to a stile in the right corner. Over this stile turn left and follow the left hedge. Ignore a left gate after a few metres, continue to the field end and then turn right in the field. At the bottom left of the field find an old stile hidden behind a large Oak tree. Over the stile follow the left hedge for 100 metres until it ends, then turn almost half-left across the field to trees and a footbridge/stile. Climb uphill to the left of the hedge and through a gate to Patches Farm. Turn left on the farm road to reach the 'main road'. Turn right for 200 metres to arrive at the lychgate of Alfrick Church. A further 100 metres brings you to the footpath going into the churchyard at the rear of the church, and a further 50 metres will bring you to the centre of Alfrick and the post office/stores.

Alfrick is a nice little town, but is said to have a number of ghosts! Take the footpath to the east side of the church (the back of the church) and go up the banking into the graveyard. It would be a shame not to go round to the front of the church however, since the Church of St Mary Magdalene is a real gem.

From the back of the church go to the back of the graveyard and through a kissing gate hidden in the trees, and then strike off half-right (in the direction of half way along the trees on the ridge ahead). This is an old parishioners' path leading to a gate onto the lane. Turn right and follow the lane round to the left for 50 metres, and then go through a gate on the left. Go straight across the field, at right angles to the lane that you have just left. Aim for the far corner, slightly to the left, where two hedges meet at an angle. Cross the next field on the same line as the left hedge (now behind you). Aim for the far left corner of the wooden fence. Just to the right of the corner is a stile onto a minor road. Turn right. Pass two roads going off to the left. When the road you are on bears right find a bridleway off to the right. After 100 metres the route splits – take the left diagonal onto a very nice enclosed track. You are now on Crews Hill. Hope it has not been wet – this is a well-used bridleway. Apart from the thin line of trees you are walking through (with super views to your right down to the Teme valley), a

Horsham Farm

68

27

B4197

67

26

wood eventually becomes obvious on your left (just past a small cliff). When the wood on your left is replaced by open fields, still carry on the ridge. You are now on Round Hill at a height of 150 metres with rural views west and Bromyard way off in the distance.

The fields on the left give way to a Scots Pine plantation (still with a wood to your right). Keep on the ridge and go through gates to enter a field to the right. Carry on the same line. At the far end of this field are two gates on the bridleway to take the path through a hedge, but DO NOT go through them. Just before the gates is a stile on the left – go over this and ignore an immediate transverse path. Head straight downhill through the trees on a very steep path, and over a stile into a field. Cross the field to go

Alfrick Church

Knightwick Oast Houses

under a bridge of the old railway line (Worcester to Bromyard and Leominster – in the days of steam it took 26 minutes to travel from Worcester to Knightwick, with a further 16 minutes to Bromyard). At the other side of the bridge follow the line of Coalpits Wood on your left. After a while Lord's Wood also comes in from the right. Keep in the open space between the woods, and then bear left to see Knightwick House ahead. Climb the field and go to the left of the house onto an old sunken lane. Join a small access road with Knightwick church in front. Turn right on the road to the 'major' road junction.

Alt Route

28

MARTLEY

69

Berrow Farm

BERROW GREEN

PH

27

B4197

On the opposite side of the road is a stile – go over this and head half-right to go to the left of a rampant hedge. Pick up a path aiming to join the A44 road well to the left of houses. Turn right on the road. At the road junction turn left along the 'No Through Road' to the pedestrian bridge over the River Teme, and arrive at the Talbot inn.

Just past the inn turn left on a metalled track and go through a tree nursery to Ankerdine Farm, with its hops climbing poles and twin disused Oast houses (now very popular and very expensive house conversions in Kent). A particularly favourite spot of Elgar's was the stretch of the River Teme from Knightsford Bridge (300 metres east of the Talbot inn) to Ham Bridge

The start of The Great English Walk

Pudford, Crews and Malvern Hills

(northwest of Martley), and then onto the Shelsleys.

A spot of flat walking can now be enjoyed as you go through the farmyard, before turning right on a broad track to the River Teme. There is a mass of Common Nettles (*Urtica dioica*) along the river bank, and this attracts Tortoiseshell and Orange Tip butterflies. Follow the track to Horsham Farm where the flat walk ends. Go over a stile into the farmyard. Turn right, then left onto the farm exit track. Go right over a stile and cross the field to a stile in the right hedge. Over this, turn left along a hedge and bear right with a stream on your left. A stile takes you to the left stream bank. Continue uphill. After some 200 metres another stile takes you back to the right stream bank. Now aim for a signpost ahead, at the left of an electricity sub station in the coll of the hill, and onto a metalled access track. Turn right and walk 300 metres to the B4197 road.

Turn left on the B4197 to the hamlet of Berrow Green. 250 metres past the Admiral Rodney inn go left onto a house drive. After 20 metres go right over a stile into a field and head for the right of Berrow Farm in the distance. En-route you meet an access road – either walk on this or in the field to the right. At the far end of the farm, as the track swings left, take the path ahead to the left side of the hedge. At the next transverse hedge pause for thought and either —

1. follow the track onwards for 350 metres to meet an obvious earth road, and turn right for 500m to reach the B4197 road;

    or

2. turn half-right and follow the hedge to the right for three fields to reach the bend of the B4197 road. Unfortunately, in 1996, the path is blocked, but maybe Worcestershire County Council will have

cleared it by the time you read this.

Either way, having arrived at the road turn left and follow it to Martley. The town has a number of red brick Georgian houses. The church of St Peter has a red perpendicular tower, and inside has early painted wall decorations. There is a 13th century curtain pattern and ornamental borders in the chancel. It also has a display of flat tomb slabs and a 1459 alabaster tomb of one of the Mortimers who was killed in the war of the Roses. The chancel is probably medieval, and there is a very nice wooden roof. The poet C S Calverley was born in the rectory here in 1831.

Leave Martley on the B4197, passing the inn and shop, and turn left on the B4204 when the B4204 road joins from the right. Follow this road for 250 metres, taking the terraced pavement on the right on your way, then turn right on the driveway of Noak Farm. Turn left to go through the farmyard behind the big house. The path has then been diverted since the last OS map issue. Pass the barns at the rear of the house, then cross the field ahead close to the right hedge. On the same line go over a stile into the next field. Follow the left hedge. Where it ends turn half-left and aim for a stile in the distant field corner at the entrance to Hill End Farm. Turn left along the minor road to a left bend, then follow the road round for a further 100 metres before going up steps on your right, for the ridge walk on the top of Pudford Hill.

The Worcestershire Way also takes the Pudford Hill route, but when this is signed downhill ignore the sign and carry on the ridge for a superb ridge walk. The hill changes name along the route to become Rodge Hill, although you are scarcely aware of the difference in contours as you change

from one to the other. There is an abundance of St John's-wort here (*Hypericum perforatum*). Continue on the ridge to reach Cockshot Hill, yet another almost unnoticed change of hill. You will now probably hear quarry workings ahead. Shortly after the trees on your right disappear a path goes down diagonally left into the trees. *Don't* take this path, but at this point strike out right down across a field to an invisible point 200 metres below. Turn left in the middle of this large field and, keeping parallel to the ridge top trees, strike out on a north north west direction (just left of straight ahead!) to a gate onto the minor road.

Once on the road turn right for 150 metres to a road junction on the left (Camp Lane). Turn left up the lane. The large quarry workings can now be seen to the left. Pass one field boundary on your right, then after another 150 metres climb the steps and stile on the right. Head directly across the field, 150 metres left of the right side hedge. Find a gap in a cross hedge and continue on the same line across the second field. At the field top turn left towards a wood to find a stile on your right. Cross two stiles to bring you to the left of a hedge, and climb uphill again (Lippetts Farm is on your right). At the field top go over a stile into

Map labels: 29 · Quarry · Camp Lane · Cockshot Hill · Large Open Fields · 72 · 188 · Rodge Hill · Pudford Hill · 71 · The Noak · B4204 · 70 · B4197 · B4204 · PH · 28 · MARTLEY · B4197

Woodbury Hill Wood.

As you enter the wood turn right, then immediately left uphill. Follow the well signposted path as it contours uphill and goes through the earthworks of the old ancient Briton fort. The fort dates from the Iron Age. In 1401 the Welsh prince Owain Glyndwr used the fort as a base for his Welsh army. He advanced to St Johns to the east, but then withdrew to the fort. Henry IV's army faced him on Abberley Hill, but only skirmishes took place and Glyndwr retreated to the Welsh hills.

Carry on the straight forest track, initially lined with Scots Pines. Follow the main track downhill, ignoring all turns off. The track eventually narrows to a path to drop down to a minor road. Turn left, and over a brook, for 30 metres to a stile on the right. Walk across the field, with a fence to the right. When you reach a stile over a fence turn left. Follow this fence initially, then carry on the same line when it ends. Aim for stiles in the middle of non-existent field boundaries, all the time aiming further for a large building on the road. Cross a footbridge at one point and reach a stream. Follow the left stream bank to reach the busy A443 road. You now discover that the 'large house' is in fact the Hundred House – an inn!

Great Witley is a 'spread out' village. The main houses are to the left, but to the right are two points of especial interest worth a detour if you have the time. Some 2km east on the A443 road is Witley Court. This was one of Europe's largest and richest Victorian palaces. The present palace, and its older predecessor, has been the home of the Foleys, Queen Adelaide (widow of William IV), the Dudleys and finally Sir Herbert Smith. There was a disastrous fire in 1937 and the property was abandoned. The Court has recently seen

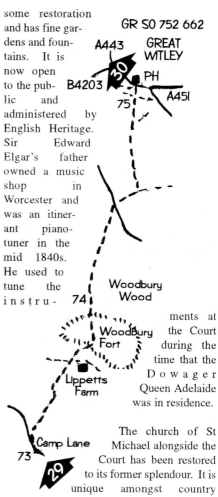

some restoration and has fine gardens and fountains. It is now open to the public and administered by English Heritage. Sir Edward Elgar's father owned a music shop in Worcester and was an itinerant piano-tuner in the mid 1840s. He used to tune the instruments at the Court during the time that the Dowager Queen Adelaide was in residence.

The church of St Michael alongside the Court has been restored to its former splendour. It is unique amongst country churches in Britain, with exquisite gilded decorations and was built for the Foley family. The interior walls and ceiling are adorned with superb baroque papier-mache work by Bagutti. There are Antonio Bellucci paintings on the ceiling and windows by Joshua Price. The organ has connections with Handel. It has the grandest baroque church interior in Britain and is open to visitors.

FIVE
Great Witley - Tenbury Wells
(13.75 miles or 22 km)

Go west along the pavement on the A443 road from the Hundred House. Pass the B4203 turn off to Bromyard, and after a further 50 metres cross the road onto the track opposite. Go along the track and through a gate. Bear right on the track, then left in front of a small pool, and follow the broad track uphill. Pass some barns in the trees on the left, but keep on the same track and curve right uphill to reach the Abberley Hall extension. The hall is an Italianate mansion, built for a Geneva banker in 1846 on the site of an earlier building. The building passed to Joseph Jones (a Lancashire mill owner) and his cousin John Joseph Jones built the clock tower in 1883 – the exact reason for its erection is unknown. Abberley was also the home of the poet William Walsh, and it is probable that his friends Dryden and Addison stayed with him in the early 18th century. The hall is now a boys preparatory school.

Keep on the track, with the buildings on the right, to meet a transverse track. Turn right for 50 metres, then left on a broad track (towards Home Farm). NB, there is no public access, but the clock tower makes a fine picture from the track.

200 metres further brings you to the School Menagerie with some cute animals. Carry on the track, and later – when the track bears right to Home Farm – go off to the left onto a footpath. There are barns in the trees to your right. Go to left of the fence across open fields until you reach a stile on the right, just before a wood. ***Don't*** cross, but turn left here and walk across the field at right angles to the fence to reach a stile on the far side. Then turn 30 degrees right across the next field to trees surrounding a small pond. Ignoring the gate to the right, keep to the left of the pond and then go to the right of two houses and cross their access drive via two gates. Cross a small field at right angles to the road, then go 45 degrees left to start a slight descent of the contours to a stile. Aim to pass to the right of a dozen Oak trees. Cross a stile into a large field. Initially, follow a line of Wild Cherry trees on your left. The trees slowly change to

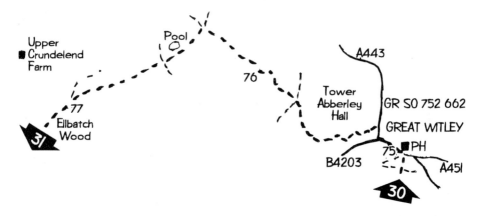

Rowmedley Farm

River Leadon

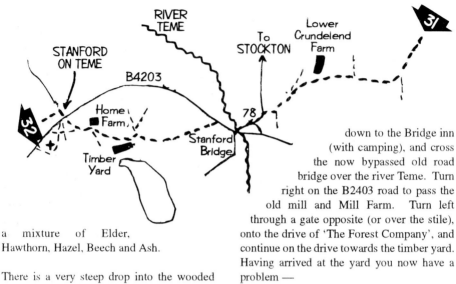

a mixture of Elder, Hawthorn, Hazel, Beech and Ash.

There is a very steep drop into the wooded valley of Meneatt Wood on the left. When a path goes down left into the wood strike out 45 degrees right to cut out the field corner, then continue following the left tree line. Eventually a farm track appears on the left, and you go to join it as the trees disappear. Turn right on the track, with a field now to the left. As you draw level with Lower Crundelend Farm on the left, turn to cross the field – aiming for 20 metres to the left of the house. At the corner of the house garden drop down to a farm access track below. Turn left and follow this to a minor road. Turn left again

Abberley Tower

down to the Bridge inn (with camping), and cross the now bypassed old road bridge over the river Teme. Turn right on the B2403 road to pass the old mill and Mill Farm. Turn left through a gate opposite (or over the stile), onto the drive of 'The Forest Company', and continue on the drive towards the timber yard. Having arrived at the yard you now have a problem —

1. the official right of way is to walk straight into the timber yard going carefully right, taking extreme care of the fork lift trucks in the yard. Wade through the seeping creosote to get to the far side of the yard, and down steps to the right of the sewerage treatment plant. At the other side of the plant go over a stile into a field and straight ahead to the left side of Home Farm.

This route is unsatisfactory. The company have tried to divert the path so that

2. just before the entrance to the yard is a new stile to the right. Cross the stile, keeping to the left of the field until you finally reach the limit of the timber yard, which is the boundary of the company's land. You are now faced with a barbed wire fence between yourself and the field. Get over the fence and make your way half-right to the left side of Home Farm on the hillock ahead.

Neither of the above routes are satisfactory,

and it is hoped that Worcestershire County Council will be able to soon sort out a common sense route.

Having arrived at Home Farm go over a stile, and head half-right to a track at the base of the hill on which the small church stands. Exit the field via a gate onto the road.

Cross over to the road heading for Orleton and Eastham. After 10 metres turn left on to a track which is followed into Bickenham Wood. The track ends at a house on the left and then continues as a path into the wood. Hope that the weather has not been wet since this is another well used bridlepath. When the wood ends the bridleway goes left, but the GEW carries straight on the same line to a distant hedge, through a gate, slightly right across the next field, and then through another gate. Broomy Fields Farm is now to the right. Head to the left side of the farm over a stile. Turn left on the farm access track, and after a few metres go right through a horse

gate. Then turn half-left across fields to another gate, then half-right down towards the Hanley Dingle Wood. Two more gates take you into the wood to pass to the right of the small Collier's pool. Climb up a field with a wood on your left, then bend left with the fence/hedge to pass to the left of a large house and onto a track. The track leads you to Hanley Court. Once a Gentlemans farm, this is now just a large farmhouse.

Walk past the Court to a 'road junction'. Take the left road to pass part of the old outbuildings of the Court, and over a stile at the track end into a field. Now head directly for the tower of All Saints Church at Hanley William, passing Church Farm before you arrive.

James Wakeman Newport is buried at the church. He owned Hanley Court and died aged 74 in 1834. He was Colonel of the Worcestershire Regiment for 40 years (and presumably saw service in the Napoleonic

Home Farm

Near Payford Bridge

Hanley Court

wars). The church dates from about 1150.

On leaving the church turn left along the road for 150 metres, then right through a gate. Head across the field at right angles to arrive to the right of a tree line. After crossing a stile go downhill, aiming at first for the left of Broach Farm. Cross a footbridge and change direction to go to the right of the farm. Turn left in front of the farmhouse and head off along the farm access road. Just after the last barn on the right turn diagonally right through a gate, and into a field – which should be crossed uphill to the far right-hand corner.

Then go over stiles and head to the left of Hurcott Farm. A water tower can now be seen, and you should head well to its right. Hurcott Farm access track is now to the right. You should aim to converge with this at the hedge ahead.

Over to your left at this point is an unusual sight in these parts – a triangulation point – at 245 metres.

Continue on the path to meet the B4204 road. Turn right on the road for a short distance to the Tally-Ho inn. Having suitably partaken of refreshment go over the stile out of the inn car park (between the inn and the road). Head down the field about 25 metres from the trees on the right, and maintain this line as the trees start to recede. You are aiming to arrive 100 metres to the right of Hill Farm. The radar dome can now be seen on the top of Titterstone Clee Hill to the north. The hill is 533 metres and the highest point yet on the walk – but first you have to get to Tenbury Wells before turning north. Ahead to the west the horizon is filled with the distant Welsh hills.

Having reached a farm track at the far side of Hill farm, turn half-left up a slight ridge and go diagonally across the field to the far corner. Cross over a stile and, on the same line, go down to a gate and

marks the position of a footbridge in the valley bottom. There is a mysterious four metre tall concrete tower on the far side. Head uphill to the right of the fence. At the top is a stile over a fence with several footpath signs. Cross over, turn right, and contour approximately 10 metres to its left to drop down and find a stile giving access into another field

Map labels: 33 — Church Farm — Broach Farm — Hurcott — 82 — HANLEY WILLIAM — B4204 — Hill Farm — PH — 34 — 83

after about 100 metres. Over this keep the hedge to your left as you walk through the field, but after some 250 metres there is a large tree plantation of non-native conifers on the left side of the hedge. The path is now re-routed over a stile into the plantation. Through the trees is yet another stile into an open field. Follow the left fence to reach a farm track. There is an unnamed old house to the left, and a direction sign. Turn *left* on the track for 20 metres, then right on a good track and through a Cherry orchard to Norgrove house.

steps into the garden of the Old Parsonage to arrive at the small village of Hanley Child.

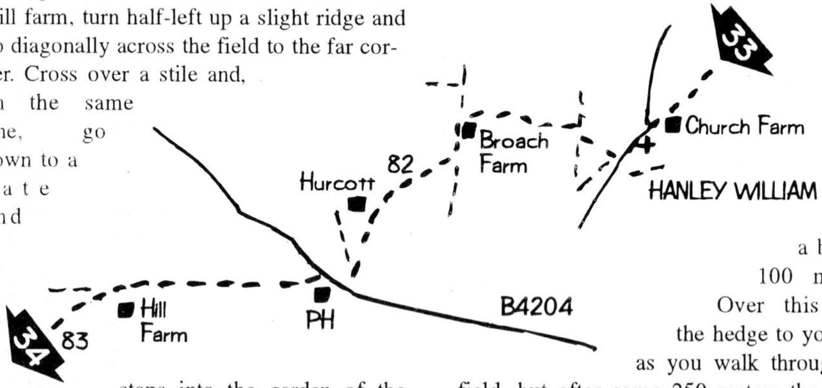

Walk forward on the tarmac road through the village. At a road junction ignore the left turn and carry on past the church of St Michael and All Angels on the right (which, according to its sign is in Hanley Childe – at some time over the years the village changed its name).

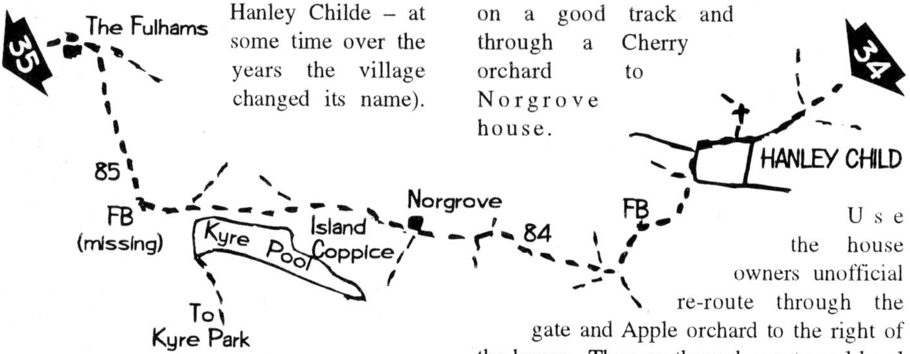

Map labels: 35 — The Fulhams — 85 — FB (missing) — Kyre Pool — Island Coppice — Norgrove — 84 — FB — HANLEY CHILD — 34 — To Kyre Park

Use the house owners unofficial re-route through the gate and Apple orchard to the right of the house. Then go through a gate and head off on a good forest track slightly downhill for 250 metres to another gate. Turn right onto a bridleway track, and after a short time

You now reach a more 'major' road. Turn left for 50 metres and then head down the field into the valley. A line of tall Poplar trees

exit this track to the right into a field. Just inside this field the bridleway splits off right, and the footpath goes left.

Take the footpath down the left side of the field, which runs parallel to the track you were on previously. Gradually views open up of Kyre Pool on the far side of that track – tantalising, but private! You finally reach a track on which you can go left to see the dam and the extent of the beautiful Kyre Pool, but your way lies ahead across the track into an almost impenetrable wood.

If you fancy a diversion at this point – and have half a day to spare – then from the dam you could carry on south on the broad track to

the B4214, then cross and make for Kyre Park garden (about 1.7km – times two if you intend to return!). The gardens are open every day from Easter to the end of October and have 29 acres (nearly 12 hectares) of gardens and shrubbery, with lakes and waterfalls. The garden houses what is probably the largest collection of hardy ferns in the world.

Back to the wood which is about 250 metres wide. The map shows a footbridge at the far side. Ah well! Fight your way through the wood at right angles to the track, and cross the stream at the far side as best you can. Having battled your way through you reach a field at the far stream side, hopefully just to the left of a hedge going in the same direction. Head up this field aiming for approximately 100 metres to the right of 'The Fulhams'. Turn left on the access track to pass to the right of the converted farm build-

Route from Tally-Ho Inn

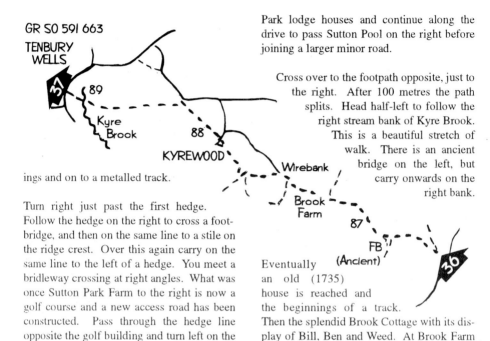

GR SO 591 663
TENBURY WELLS
89
Kyre Brook
88
KYREWOOD
Wirebank
Brook Farm
87
FB
(Ancient)
36

Park lodge houses and continue along the drive to pass Sutton Pool on the right before joining a larger minor road.

Cross over to the footpath opposite, just to the right. After 100 metres the path splits. Head half-left to follow the right stream bank of Kyre Brook. This is a beautiful stretch of walk. There is an ancient bridge on the left, but carry onwards on the right bank.

ings and on to a metalled track.

Turn right just past the first hedge. Follow the hedge on the right to cross a footbridge, and then on the same line to a stile on the ridge crest. Over this again carry on the same line to the left of a hedge. You meet a bridleway crossing at right angles. What was once Sutton Park Farm to the right is now a golf course and a new access road has been constructed. Pass through the hedge line opposite the golf building and turn left on the golf course drive. Pass No 1 and No 2 Sutton

Eventually an old (1735) house is reached and the beginnings of a track. Then the splendid Brook Cottage with its display of Bill, Ben and Weed. At Brook Farm carry on the track for a further 400 metres

Kyrewood House

East from Ragged Stone Hill

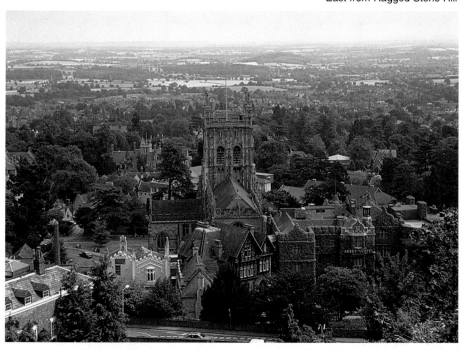

Descent to Malvern Priory

then, just before Wirebank Cottage, a bridle-way goes off to the left. Then, opposite the house, is a stile that you are looking for. Over the stile head half-right across a field to a stile into trees, and another stile to join a track coming up from a house down to the left. Turn right up the track for a stiff contouring climb. At the top go over a stile on the left and head out across a field, aiming to be on the right of the hedge ahead to arrive at the hamlet of Kyrewood.

Take the stile on the left onto a road. Turn right for 25 metres, then left at a sign to 'Field Engineering Company'. Head for the back of the old barns and turn right onto a track. Then, as the fields start, find a stile on the right and go to the far left field corner (just to the left of the house with the very large windows). Enter onto a short green lane to the B4204 road.

Turn immediately left onto a track which heads directly for Tenbury Wells. Initially the track goes through a large Currant bush plantation. The track peters out to a path, still aiming direct for Tenbury Wells. The path is clear and eventually joins a wide track. Turn left and go over the stepping stones over Kyre Brook, and up to a metalled footpath which joins the A4112 road at the Pembroke House inn. Turn right to walk along Cross Street, Market Street and Teme street on the way to the north end of Tenbury Wells, and the

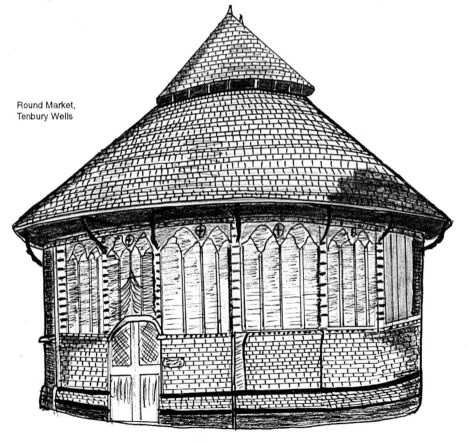

Round Market,
Tenbury Wells

River Teme.

The town used to be surrounded by orchards, but these have now sadly diminished in extent, has have also the widespread Hop yards (which Kent calls Hop fields).

The Victoria and Albert Museum in London houses the Worcestershire tapestry made in the reign of Elizabeth I —

From whence sweet springs do flowe
Whose moistur good doth firtil make
the valleis couchte belowe
Heare goodly orchards planted are
In fruite which doo abounde
Thine ey wolde make thine hart rejoyce
To see so pleasant ground.

Tenbury used to have a pump room in the 1800s when it was a spa town. The room closed in 1939, but there are hopes that some restoration work will be carried out in the future. In 1863 the charges at the pump room were —

Warm bath	2/6d
Course of 9 baths	£1
Warm shower bath	2/-
A cold shower bath	1/6d
A cold bath	1/6d
A course of 7 cold baths	10/-

A royal charter was granted to the town by Henry III on the 8th January 1249 *"of a weekly market on Tuesday at his manor of Temettebury and of a yearly fair there on the vigil and the feast of the translation of St Thomas the Martyr"*.

The medieval bridge over the River Teme at the north end of the town was strengthened and widened by Thomas Telford in 1815, not long after his success in building the famous bridge over the Menai Straits in 1812. The bridge spans the boundary between Worcestershire and Shropshire, and was extensively repaired after flood damage in 1908. The River Teme has a long history of flooding the town. Its source is in the Welsh hills, and after heavy rain has flooded the town many times, particularly in 1946 and 1947.

The Royal Oak inn is largely Jacobean, but could be older. The name derives from the Oak tree in which Charles II hid after his escape from the battle of Worcester.

In the town centre is the round market built in 1862 (but which is actually oval).

The Ship inn in Teme Street is particularly worthy of note. It was a farm until 1729, when it was converted to an inn. In horse riding days, before the motor car, it used to boast accommodation for 100 horses. Now it is a very pleasant inn renowned for excellent food.

The railway was built between 1859 and 1864. The line was closed in the 'Beeching Cuts' – westward in 1961, and eastward in 1963. Goods continued until 1965. The railway was partially built on the remains of a canal started in 1793, to go from Kington to Stourport.

SIX
Tenbury Wells - Clee Hill
(6 miles or 9.6 km)

This section of the GEW is very short, but is the most difficult and demanding stage.

The paths, of course, should all be there and in a reasonable walking condition. *But* the situation on the ground is very different. The walk should be through attractive countryside, with Titterstone Clee Hill gradually getting closer.

Just before you leave Tenbury Wells pause to look at the plaque, on the wall of the restaurant opposite the Ship inn. Dr Henry Hill Hickman was the first doctor in the UK to experiment with, and use, anaesthesia. Born in Bromyard, he practised in Tenbury Wells, but had a short life between 1800 and 1830. You may well need some smelling salts attempting to walk the present state of paths going north.

The start of the section is clear enough. Walk along Teme Street to the Teme bridge. Halfway across you leave Worcestershire and enter Shropshire, so the Tenbury Wells inhabitants to the north of the river live in a different county to those on the south side. In Roman times they called the area *Salop,* but when shires were created about AD 900 the county was initially called *Scobbesbyrigscir.* Arriving at the north end of the bridge, turn left on the A456 road (the Swan hotel is on the opposite side of the road). Walk past the conical mound of Castle Tump on the left. There are a number of legends surrounding its origin, from a Bronze age burial mound, to the last resting place of Caractacus (but that seems more likely to be in Rome), to a Norman keep. Nobody knows the real story. Take the second road on the right (the B4214

to Clee Hill). The Rose and Crown inn is on the corner (Tenbury seems particularly well served with places of refreshment!). At last, as you turn the corner you are heading north again, after the previous east to west section.

Pass the Wells soft drinks factory, and cross the railway bridge (the old abandoned line from Woofferton to Kidderminster, when it used to take 49 minutes from Kidderminster to Tenbury Wells, or another 10 minutes onwards to Woofferton, where you could change to get to Shrewsbury or Hereford). Turn left on the minor road signposted 'Greete and Whitton', then immediately right over a padlocked gate.

This first path section is in need of attention, but is not too bad to walk. Head across the field with house gardens to your right. Carry on this line as the houses and road recede farther away to the right. Go through a gate and a barbed wire fence, and then an old broken stile on the right bank of a small stream. There is some more wire, then head to the right of the house ahead (Greenwayhead house). Arrive at the fenced off house drive, but don't cross this fence. Climb uphill, parallel to the drive, to reach a gate and pass through onto the drive. Continue uphill to the main B4214 road.

Turn left on the road for 400 metres to reach a road junction (signposted The Round Oak) at the hamlet of Rugpits. The sign on the house gable end proclaims that the houses were built in 1859.

Carry on the road for a further 300 metres until a sign indicates that you have reached

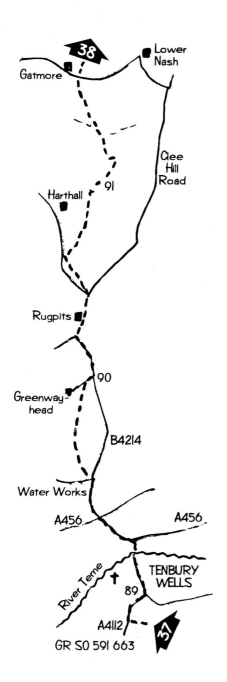

the hamlet of Nash, mentioned in the *Domesday Book* under the name of *Esses* which means "at the Ash tree". A road goes off left here to Harthall.

Here you must, at present, make a decision on which route to take. A glance at the map shows Gatmore some 1.5km to the north. There is a path to Gatmore, but at present it is very difficult. North from Gatmore is another series of paths via Mahorall Farm to Knowlegate, only about a third of which is anything like possible to walk. We must hope that with time, and enough complaints, the Shropshire County Council will find the resources to make the public rights of way walkable. The choices from Nash to Gatmore are therefore —

1. in the corner of the field at the junction between the minor road to Harthall and the B4214 road is a gate. Go through the gate, and go to the left of the garden of Nash House on your right. You are heading across a field towards a junction of minor roads at Harthall. As you descend to the stream to the right of this junction you will need to negotiate a wire fence, then turn right to go along the right bank of the stream. Go through a gate and try to follow the stream on your left side. Following this stream will involve climbing barbed wire fences on the way. Then break through a hedge line to reach a partially dried out pool one field to the east of Harthall itself (a very large house to the left).

Pass to the right of the pool, then you will see a field hedge on your left. You can try to climb over the water trough to get to the left side of this hedge line, or you can continue on the right side of this hedge to pass a well –and go through a gate after about 200 metres – to get to the left side of the hedge. So far this path has been something of a farce, but as you reach the far end of this field there is a new stile! Turn left over this for 100 metres to another new stile leading into a very large field. Then turn half-right and make your way to a lonely tree in the centre of this enormous field. Officially the path goes to a point half way between this tree and the right side hedge, then turns left for the large lonely Oak tree.

Having got to this lonely outpost, pause again for thought. Again, officially, the path now heads northwest in the direction of the farm you can see ahead (Cotterill Farm, to the north of Gatmore). Having made the decision to go on, start to head in that direction, aiming for the tree line below. You first have to negotiate barbed wire and a stream through the trees, then a fence into the field beyond. Then head diagonally left towards a stream, and Gatmore House on the road below. You need to arrive on this road just to the right of the stream via more barbed wire.

Once you have arrived at this point, there should be more paths north to Knowlegate, but the advice at present must be to turn right and walk to the B4214 road;

or

2. from the road junction at Nash, walk on the little used road north to the minor road going off left to Gatmore. A distance of some 1.7km, and very much easier than the path route.

From here there really is only one option at present, and that is to continue walking on the road to Knowlegate. Continue on this road, therefore, for 2km to pass Lower Nash farm to the left, then a junction where two roads go off right, and continue north to Knowlegate.

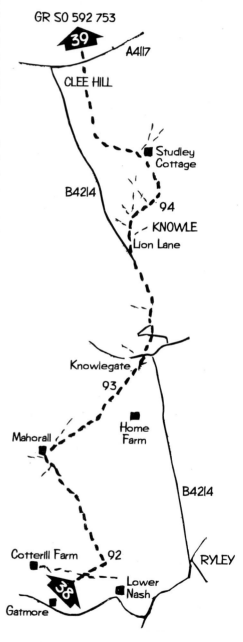

The official GEW route is to continue north from Gatmore House on the right bank of the stream, before crossing a tributary to head northwest to Mahorall Farm. Then its northeasterly to the road junction at Knowlegate, but this route at present is well and truly blocked.

Once at Knowlegate you might be forgiven for thinking the worst was over, but not so. At the road junction there should be a path to the right of the house, heading straight up through the wood, and crossing the hairpin bends of the road as it climbs up to Clee Hill, but again at present these paths are blocked.

For the time being, until the paths are made walkable, follow the B4214 to the right and climb up its hairpin bends – taking extreme care of traffic, although fortunately it is not a busy road. Once you have left the bends there is a sign for a recycling point off to the left, and then 150 metres on the right is tarmaced Lion Lane (with a bridleway sign).

Turn along the lane for 300 metres until it turns left. At this point turn right over a cattle grid. There are now three routes from which to choose – one goes uphill to the left, one straight on, and one in the middle. Take the middle track to climb gently, then bear left.

The area is full of old miners' tracks, and this is one of them. Look out for the viaduct some 300 metres to the right (no, it's not an old railway bridge, it's a more modern structure to carry water from reservoirs in Wales to the east to the midland towns). Carry on the track as it starts to climb, to the point where there

are two houses on your right (Fearnside and Studley Cottage). Just before Studley Cottage branch off diagonally left on a track up the hillside. Just to your left here is a triangulation point, or so it seems. In fact it is a marker put in by the water board to show where their major water pipe is buried. Another path joins from the left and the track splits. Head left up a slightly sunken old cart track to reach a fence. Turn right along the fence and proceed to the A4117 road at Clee Hill.

There is sometimes confusion over the names of the hills. The town you are now in is Clee Hill. To the north is the rise of Titterstone Clee Hill at 533 metres (1,750 feet). To the north of that is Brown Clee Hill, but this encompasses a number of 'peaks'. First is Clee Burf at 510 metres (1,675 feet), then Abdon Burf at 540 metres (1,773 feet) – this is the highest point in Shropshire.

The hills dominate the landscape in this eastern part of Shropshire. Mining has been carried on here since the 16th century in the search for Iron, Basalt, Limestone and Copper. A restraining factor, however, was the difficulty of transport to the main town areas.

In 1864 the transport problem was solved when the Ludlow and Clee Hill Railway was built, as a branch line from the main Shrewsbury to Hereford line. The line ran initially to Bitterley (2.5km west of the top of the hill), but was extended to Clee Hill top in 1867.

The line was opened as a mineral line only – officially there were no passengers.

SEVEN
Clee Hill - Longville in the Dale
(16.75 miles or 26.8 km)

Opposite to where you arrived at Clee Hill, on the A4117 road, is a small lane. Go onto this lane to pass Victoria Cottage after 100 metres, then turn left through a gate onto a broad track. To your right up the slight rise is the Kremlin inn (with a Russian inverted 'R'). You are now on one of the old railway tracks in the area. You may be lucky and see a Golden Plover. The track passes slowly disintegrating loading bays on the right, bends right, and arrives at a minor road at the Hedgehog House, complete with its post box and telephone kiosk.

Turn right for 25 metres on the road, then go through a gate on the left. The radar domes can now be seen on the top of Titterstone Clee Hill. Cross the field with a fence to your right, and continue over a stile to the bottom of the field and a gate. Turn right through the gate. You are now, for some distance, on the same route as the Shropshire Way. Go through the gate and turn right, following the fence on the right to a stile. Over this stile head diagonally left across the field, to a stile a little left of the hedge on the far side. Through the stile follow the right fence until you reach Nine Springs Farm. *Don't* go through the gate, but turn left down the field to the bottom corner. Go through the gate and turn right to the footbridge over Benson's Brook. Beyond the brook go left uphill and cross a farm track, then cross the small moor to the bridge carrying the old railway incline.

Clee Hill Rail Incline

Climb the embankment, before the bridge, and up to the inclined track.

The incline opened on the 1st June 1867, and locomotives took over from horses ten years later to shunt wagons on the level quarry floor, before they were let down the incline. The incline was unique in having a three rail system – the centre rail being 'common' for ascending and descending wagons. The incline was actually 1,988 yards long (1,816 metres), and had a gradient of over 1 in 9. Wagons were lowered with a 4.5 inch (114mm) wire rope, and the load was restricted to 85 tons. At its peak 6,000 tons of stone each week were dispatched, and the quarry employed 2,000 people (which probably means it supported over 10,000 people locally). The line, however, was not the only means of moving materials. A 3.5 mile (5.6km) aerial ropeway was used for a time to take material eastwards, down to the Cleobury Mortimer and Ditton Priors Railway, as well as some stone being dispatched by road. The rail line and quarry closed on the 7th November 1960.

Climb up the track to its head, where the quarry floor has a very large amount of broken concrete structures. This is all that remains of the vast quarry workings. Turn half-right up the gradual rise of an old quarry track, and follow this as it bears left to meet the Radar Station road at a hairpin bend. The road is lined with many roadside reflectors, which must be

essential on a bleak dark winter's night. Cross the hairpin, turn 30 metres to the right, then left up a well used track to the ridge. From here you can look down into the vast quarry floor. Turn left to the open radars, ie. the flat radar protectors to the left. The station is operated by the National Air Services. Go left up to the triangulation point at 533 metres. To the west you can see Ludlow less than 9km away, with the Welsh hills beyond. The main sight is to the north, to Brown Clee Hill – your next objective!

When you have done feasting your eyes on the views, turn east to go to the left of the larger radar dome, then turn NNE (towards Brown Clee) and head downhill. You are aiming for the red roof of Callowgate Farm way below. Once you have crossed the open moor and arrived at the fence before the farmhouse, ***Don't*** cross, but turn left along the fence to a gate giving access to an old farm track. This is a long track, which becomes more distinct, and even has a name – Callow Lane. The track passes a pool on the right, a barn on the left, and a plantation on the right before arriving at a minor road near Bromdon Farm. Turn left on the road for 200 metres. A path goes off to the right to Wheathill youth hostel. Carry on the road for a further 500 metres to reach the farm access road of Knapp Farm on the left. Turn down the track towards the farm, but just before the farm's garden turn

40

Callowgate

98

533
Titterstone
Clee Hill   97   Radar
                         Dome
             Quarry

Incline

FB
Nine Springs
Farm

96

Hedgehog
House

Disused
Railway

95

CLEE HILL
GR SO 592 753   39

Radar Domes and Quarry

right and follow the fence. Go over the stile at the bottom of the field, cross the stream and continue to the gate alongside the house ahead. Turn left along the house drive to arrive at the B4364 road. Turn right for 20 metres, then left along the farm road to Newton. Just before Newton Farm the road gradually bears round to the right, over a stream, and then starts to climb. A house on the right is the limit of the 'road', which then degenerates into a green lane and climbs to the minor road (Thorn Lane, which goes from Blackford to Stoke St Milborough – the latter is 2.3km to the west, with the famous St Milburga's Well which is said to cure eye complaints).

Go straight across the road and continue on a sunken green lane. Pass over a new access road from The Mill Farm, then bear right on a green lane and onto a path through a Gorse thicket. You are climbing all the time. Go through a gate at the start of a wood on your right (Old Lodge coppice). The path soon bears left to carry you across the open moor to the communication mast ahead on Clee Burf. You are now at 510 metres. There used to be a settlement here centuries ago – a very cold and remote place to live! Once you arrive at the mast the public right of way ends. However, there is a path established by long usage which goes through the gate to the right of the mast, and then along the ridge, with Castle Covert wood to your right. You shortly arrive at a dip known as 'The Five Springs'. Whether there are actually five springs is up to you to judge!

The terrain now falls away rapidly to the west into a valley. 2km to the west is the hamlet of Cockshutford, and just to its south is Nordybank Iron Age hill fort. The fort is well preserved with good ramparts and ditches (there were also Iron Age hill forts on Abdon Burf and Clee Burf, but quarrying and other diggings have left little remains of these).

Whilst the entire area is called Brown Clee, there are two peaks. You have just passed Clee Burf at 510 metres, and you can now see Abdon Burf ahead, complete with its (almost compulsory) radio mast. From the dip of Five Springs head in a north westerly direction, ie. aim for the flank of the hill to the left of the masts on Abdon Burf. You shortly reach a gate, on the other side of which are two paths. One goes just to the right of a fence, but the other (which you should take) heads uphill towards the masts. Go uphill on the track and reach a fence corner at Sandy Nap. Carry on to the right of this fence line until you are almost level with the masts where you will find a stile on the left.

You can make a detour to the trig point if you wish. The pillar is at 540 metres and is the highest point in the whole of Shropshire. The views west over Wenlock Edge to Caer Caradoc and the Welsh hills are extensive.

The masts carry vertical dishes. These are microwave transmitters/receivers. Many years ago British Telecom started to use this form of transmission to supplement their underground cables. Before World War II BT was using a form of transmission known as 'Carrier' which enabled them to pack first 12, then 24 conversations down one pair of wires. Then came coaxial cables and equipment which meant that

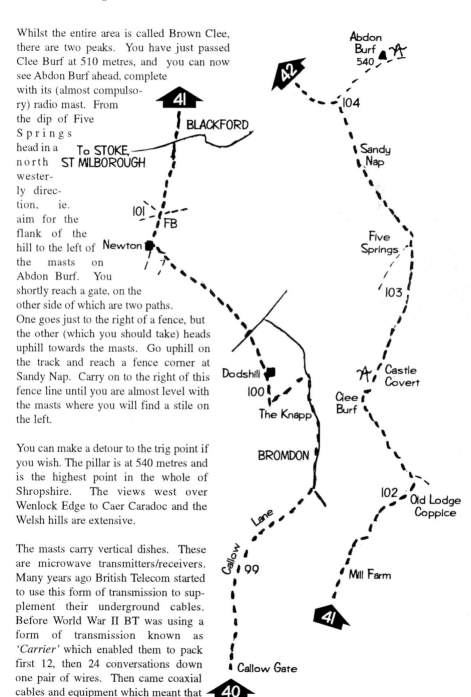

Abdon Burf 540

104

BLACKFORD

To STOKE ST MILBOROUGH

Sandy Nap

101

FB

Newton

Five Springs

103

Dodshill

Castle Covert

100

The Knapp

Clee Burf

BROMDON

102 Old Lodge Coppice

Lane

Callow

99

Mill Farm

41

Callow Gate

40

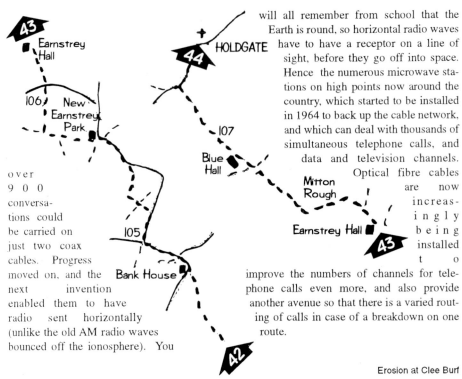

will all remember from school that the Earth is round, so horizontal radio waves have to have a receptor on a line of sight, before they go off into space. Hence the numerous microwave stations on high points now around the country, which started to be installed in 1964 to back up the cable network, and which can deal with thousands of simultaneous telephone calls, and data and television channels. Optical fibre cables are now increasingly being installed to improve the numbers of channels for telephone calls even more, and also provide another avenue so that there is a varied routing of calls in case of a breakdown on one route.

over 9 0 0 conversations could be carried on just two coax cables. Progress moved on, and the next invention enabled them to have radio sent horizontally (unlike the old AM radio waves bounced off the ionosphere). You

Erosion at Clee Burf

To continue the walk go back to the fence line and over the stile. Then, as you start to go downhill, there is a second stile on the left to reach the start of a sunken lane. This lane goes downhill and bears right for some distance to meet a minor metalled road at Bank House. Turn right for 200 metres to a road junction, then left for 250 metres to another road junction, then turn right towards Earnstrey (to the south lies the village of Abdon, with the site of the old medieval village of Abdon nearby). After a further 200 metres on the road there is a stile on the left. Go over this and cross the field with the fence/hedge to the left. At the end of the field turn right to complete two field sides and go over a footbridge. Bear half-left up a small lane to join a minor road. Turn left along this road for 300 metres and, just before New Earnstrey Farm, take the stile on the left. Go down the farm side, then right over a stile, and count two full fields on the right side after you leave the farm buildings. Turn right through the fence to head towards the road, changing fence/hedge sides after the first field. Follow the hedge on your left in

the last field, but note that the stile to the road is 50 metres from the left corner.

Cross the road and walk up the drive of Earnstrey Hall. After passing the hall go through one gate, cross a field with a fence on the left and go through a second gate. Almost immediately turn left through a third gate. This brings you above Mittons Rough Wood. Keep on this side of the wood until it ends, and then continue in the same direction on a path to the right of a line of Hawthorn bushes for 150 metres. Turn right down the contours to the stile you will see at the base of the hill. Head for a point 300 metres south (left) of Holdgate Church.

Cross fields to pass to the right of Blue Hall (a small house) where you swop over to the left of a hedge. Follow the footpath signs which lead to the right of Holdgate Farm and onto a minor road. Turn right to Holy Trinity Church at Holdgate. The village lies in Corve Dale, a shallow valley to the east of Wenlock Edge.

In the *Domesday Book* the village was called *Stanton,* but changed to Holdgate – derived from the Norman landowner Helgot. Helgot built a castle here, but only the earthworks still remain (behind the church). The *Domesday Book* also says that a church existed here before the Norman conquest, which would make the original church very old. The oldest part of the present church dates from

Wilderhope Manor YHA 45

110

Lower Stanway

109

B4368

Rowe Lane

108

HOLDGATE

44

the 13th century (chancel and tower). There are some 14th century windows, and the font is 12th century.

AE Housman was a famous Shropshire novelist and poet. He described this area —

Wenlock Edge was umbered
And bright was Abdon Burf
And warm between them slumbered
The smooth green miles of turf.

Pass through the gate to the left of the church, and head down the field to a stile 100 metres to the left of the pool. Then follow the left fence for some distance to a stile and stepping stones over Trow Brook. Continue on the same line, now to the left of a hedge, to a minor road (Rowe Lane). Go directly across the road and through a gate, then turn left along the hedge for 100 metres to reach a fence. Don't cross this fence, but turn right through two fields ignoring a stile on the left halfway through the second field. Cross a footbridge and turn right to the field corner, then left to climb the field to the B4368 road.

GR SO 539 938
LONGVILLE IN THE DALE

Longville Arms
46
B4371
45

From the top of Brown Clee, Wenlock Edge was very distinctive as a ridge going diagonally from southwest to northeast, halfway to the hills of Caer Caradoc and the Lawleys, but now that you are here it is difficult to find much of a hill. The Edge was formed as a Coral reef in a tropical sea 420 million years ago. Turn right for a few metres, then left on the road leading to Longville in the Dale. Just after the first bend go over a stile on the right and down to a bridge (the access track for New House). Turn immediately left to go along the right bank of the unnamed tributary of the River Corve. Keep

Wilderhope Manor

on this bank of the stream until just below Lower Stanway Farm, when a diversion takes the track to the other side and to the farm access track. Turn right over the track bridge, then left on the right stream bank again. The path changes sides a number of times from here on its way to Wilderhope Manor, but the path is always clear.

Wilderhope Manor is finally seen, and the track passes to the right, and front, of the manor. The house was built sometime before 1590 for Thomas Smallman and owned by his family until 1742. There is a story of one of his descendants, another Thomas Smallman, who was a Royalist during the English Civil War. He was imprisoned by the troops of Cromwell, but escaped on horseback by jumping over a point known as Major's Leap, near Stretton Westwood 7km to the northeast. The house has beautiful plaster ceilings and a solid wooden staircase. Although owned by the National Trust, the house is leased to the YHA as a hostel.

Carry on the straight track in front of the manor, and then pass a very large field to the left. When you reach a hedge/fence going off at right angles to the left, turn left (and leave the Shropshire Way). Follow the hedge and climb up to the trees on the top of Wenlock Edge. Go left through a stile (into National Trust land), and immediately right over another stile. Go diagonally downhill through the trees on a direct line, ignoring a transverse track. Climb a stile into a field and head half-right to a fence, on the far side of which turn left, then right at the bottom of the field, then through a gate onto the B4371 road. Turn left on the road to the bridge over the old railway line. This was the Wellington to Coalbrookdale and Craven Arms line. In the days of steam train transport you could travel from Much Wenlock to Longville in 15 minutes, and from Longville to Craven Arms in a further 22 minutes. The line was one of the many casualties of the car, and closed in the 1960s. The old station can be seen from the bridge.

Carry on over the bridge to the hamlet of Longville in the Dale.

EIGHT
Longville in the Dale - Church Stretton
(7 miles or 11.2 km)

Leave the Longville Arms inn and walk along the B4371 (in a south westerly direction) for 1.5km, then turn right on the road to East Wall. At East Wall Farm (on the right) follow the tarmac road to the left for 200 metres, then turn through the gate on the right onto a bridleway. Having passed through

over the fence. Head across the field directly at right angles, and climb another fence. Turn half-left to go through a gate to the right of Hill End Farm (you have now completed three sides of a walk around the farm buildings).

the gate ignore one left fork off the way and keep to the right of the hedge all the way to Gilberries Lane. Turn right on the lane for 550 metres – then just past the fifth field on the left, turn left onto a farm access track. At the farm go to the right of the building down to a stream, through a gate on the left, and cross the Heath Brook over a footbridge. Climb the field to the left of a hedge (a few metres into the field is a stile to the right leading to Cardington village 1km away). Follow the hedge on the right until you reach a gate one field short of Hill End Farm. There is no right of way through the

Walk past the farm environs and through a gate. Go half-right and along the base of Hill End contours, then slightly right to find a stile in the fence ahead. Aim slightly right again down to a gate onto a minor road (Cardington to Wall under Heywood). The hills of Caer Caradoc and The Lawley are now looming to the right.

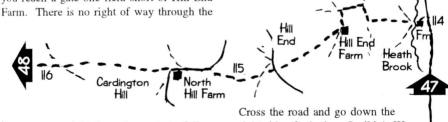

farm, so turn right through a gate to follow the hedge/fence on your left until some 30 metres short of a gate through a hedge. At this point turn left over an old footbridge and

Cross the road and go down the right side of a hedge. Ippikin's Way now runs in company with the GEW for a short time. Ippikin seems to have been something of a rogue who lived in the 13th

Caer Caradoc and The Lawley

century in a cave on Wenlock Edge, and was not fussy about stealing from others! It seems that his ghost still haunts the Edge. At the end of the first field go through a gate and turn half-right, to aim for a point 100 metres from the right bottom field corner. Cross the fence and go onto a private minor road. Turn left up the road to reach North Hill Farm.

When the road turns left after the farm, carry straight on over a stile and follow the hedge on the right. After the third field you reach a small valley carrying a small stream going off to the right. Go over the next stile, then head 30 degrees left to start going round the flank of Willstone Hill and Battle Stones. Cross a fence on the right to climb the hill flank. Abdon Burf and Titterstone

Clee Hill are very clear, but a long way behind. Follow the left fence as it takes you over Willstone Hill and down to a coll. Go over the stile and turn right downhill, then bear left with a track down the valley.

On reaching a gate turn left, heading in the direction of Church Stretton now seen below.

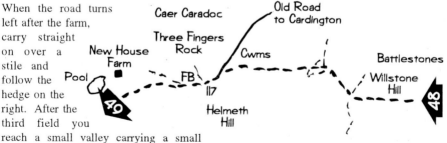

This is a difficult area for footpaths despite its popularity. Rights of way are not that well defined. *But* you eventually see a track coming in from the right – head diagonally

towards it. Once you reach the track turn left and follow it over a stream – this is the old 'road' from Church Stretton to Cardington. Shortly beyond this point is a footbridge on the right. Mark this bridge in your mind, since this is the place for the ascent of Caer Caradoc on your return from Church Stretton.

To visit Church Stretton carry on the track, and pass the heavily wooded Helmeth Hill to your left. Keep on the track until it arrives in a field and disappears!

New House Farm is down to the right. Follow the fence line on the left. A large pool (with island) has been created near the farm. There is a sunken stream on the left. The path eventually bears right down to a farm access road (part of the Cardington road again). Turn left on the now tarmaced road for 150 metres, then go over a stile on the right – carrying on the road would have brought you into the Battlefield housing estate – more about this later. Walk diagonally across to the far left field corner towards an electricity transformer mounted on two poles, then carry on past and onto the old Roman Watling Street. Cross the street, and a field to reach the modern road of the A49. What a contrast between the Roman and modern roads! Cross the busy A49 and carry on the right side of the town putting green. Cross the railway line (this is the first **_used_** line to be seen on the GEW so far, if you don't count walking over the one under the Malvern hills) and go to the right of a house to a housing estate road. Turn left along the road to the centre of Church Stretton.

The town was a demesne manor of the Earls of Mercia before the Norman invasion, and then became a manor of the Norman Earl of Shrewsbury. The name derived later from the Roman Watling Street, and could be said to mean literally "the church near the Roman road". Watling Street connected the Roman towns of *Viroconium* and *Bravinium*.

Caer Caradoc

The town stands at 190 metres and is a mecca for walkers – most of whom seem to walk the Long Mynd hills to the west of the town. The church of St Laurence has a Norman north wall with a blocked up doorway. Known as the corpse door, this was only used at funerals. There is a Celtic fertility symbol above the north doorway, and this type of ornamentation is known as a *Sheila-na-gig*. The church has a memorial to Sarah Smith who **GR SO 543 938** wrote under her pen name 'Hesba Stretton' of *Jessica's First Prayer* in 1866.

The area became known as 'Little Switzerland' in the late-19th century because of its breath-taking beauty. There is an Edwardian feel about the town, which is very pleasant. Natural spring water is bottled for sale. The valley lies in a natural fault line separating the pre-Cambrian Long Mynd from the older hills to the east, known collectively as the Stretton hills (Caer Caradoc and The Lawley etc). The Long Mynd was formed from raised sea bed sediments, but the Stretton hills are amongst the oldest in Britain having been formed from lava and ash by volcanic action 900 million years ago (and would originally have been very much higher). Church Stretton is the *Shepwardine* of Mary Webb's novels. The town has all the facilities that you could wish.

A49   Newhouse Farm
Pool
CHURCH STRETTON 118
Watling Street

Caer Caradoc from Church Stretton

NINE
Church Stretton - Shrewsbury
(18 miles or 28.8 km)

This section starts off with an invigorating climb. The poet John Masefield perhaps expressed the views of a great many people with —

There, somewhere, nor- nor- east from me
Was Shropshire where I longed to be
Ercall and Mynd
Severn, Wrekin, you and me.

From Church Stretton centre turn onto Essex Road (parallel to the rail line). Pass Ascot Close on left, then turn right on path alongside the retirement home and through the garden to a stile onto the railway line. On the far side go alongside the putting green to the A49, then cross Watling Street and return along the route you took to previously arrive at Church Stretton. You will recall that you marked a footbridge on the way to the town. On your return the bridge is not that obvious, but you reach a fork on the old Cardington Road, where the left fork goes down to the stream, and after 10 metres there is the bridge – if you reach a ford on the old Cardington Road, you have gone about 50 metres too far and need to retrace your steps.

When you have crossed

the footbridge turn right for about 50 metres, then turn left and strike straight uphill through the Gorse bushes (or rather around them!). After some 50 metres a wide path becomes obvious as you climb up this public right of way path. You soon reach a fence, with paths going off in each direction. The paths to each side are the only official paths, and you can indeed reach the top of the hill if you turn right and follow the overgrown path. However, everyone goes over the fence at this point and carries on straight uphill.

As you climb, the views become spectacular over to Church Stretton on your left and the Battlestones to your right. The summit of Caer Caradoc can be seen ahead. Three Fingers Rock is finally reached, with its rock pillars pointing skyward.

The path on the far side of the rocks goes down two small dips on the way to arrive at the summit of Caer Caradoc. At the summit are the few remains of earth embankments

Three Fingers Rock

from the Ancient Briton fort. The summit is 459 metres, which sounds much better as 1,507 feet.

Perhaps this is the point at which you should consider history. In 55BC Julius Caesar mounted his first invasion of Britain, and he invaded again in 54BC. In 43AD the Romans came to stay, and in this year came the death of Cymbeline who was the king of the British tribe Catuvellauni, and who had collaborated with the Romans. Cymbeline was succeeded by his son Caractacus, who resisted and fought the Romans. Caractacus' army was defeated by the Romans at the battle of the Medway, again in 43AD.

In 50AD Caractacus raised another army to fight the invading Romans, this time at what is known as the Battle of Shropshire. The battle took place here, or at the base of the hill in the area now known as Battlefield. The superior might of the Romans won, but

Caractacus escaped. It is interesting to reflect that everyone knows about the Norman invasion in 1066 and how they won the battle of Hastings. This place is hardly known, and yet should be equally famous as the last battle of the ancient Celtic tribes of England and Wales against the invader. The Romans never did manage to conquer the tribes of Scotland or Ireland, but this place and date should be as famous as Hastings and 1066. The Romans captured Caractacus in 51AD and put him on display in Rome, where he died in captivity in 54AD.

Ahead is the small summit of Little Caradoc, and beyond that the humpback of The Lawley. Head straight for Little Caradoc on the ridge path, following a fence on the right for part of the way. Go over a stile and then slightly to the right side of Little Caradoc to continue down the hill. Keep straight on down the ridge of the hill and into trees to reach a fence. Turn left on a path down to a track in the trees. Turn right through a gate and walk through the wood following the track to a road. Turn right on the road, and follow it as it bends to pass Caradoc House on the left. Then turn left when you meet a T-junction. This is Comley hamlet. Carry on this road for 300 metres, then turn off right onto a farm drive. Turn right again after 50 metres (at a bridleway signpost) onto a wide drive. Go over a cattle grid and after 20 metres turn right off the track to head for a gate and stile, which gives access to the ridge of The Lawley. Again this is a permissive path enabling you to climb directly up towards the summit.

The Lawley climb is not as steep as Caer Caradoc, but also gives superb views. As you climb, a black and white building comes into sight down to the west of the hill. This is Penkridge Hall.

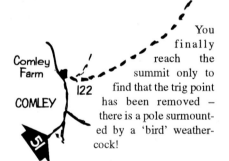

You finally reach the summit only to find that the trig point has been removed – there is a pole surmounted by a 'bird' weathercock!

There is a 'gentle' descent from the summit at 377 metres, and 1.5 km brings you to the earthworks of an ancient abandoned settlement. Carry on along the ridge, and at the very north of the hill the path descends into a wood, and over a stile to follow to the right of a fence to join a road.

Turn left on the road. Pink Purslane and Herb Robert grow in the roadside verge. Follow the road round a hairpin bend, and over a stream. The road now turns sharp left, with a

track off to the right – go over a gate directly ahead, and turn half-left to cross to the far left field corner near a solitary Oak tree. There are two gates in the corner. Choose the one on the left, go through and follow the right hedge to reach a gate giving access to a farm road at Bentley Ford Farm.

There is now a choice —

1. the GEW goes over the gate opposite, then turns half-left to the far left field corner. At this point in 1996 there is an impenetrable hedge. When Shropshire County Council install a stile, go left over it and follow the right hedge to go over another stile (also missing in 1996) onto a minor road (which was the major Roman Watling Street 2,000 years ago!) near the hamlet of Frodesley Lane. Cross the road and go over a stile (again also missing), and head in a direct line for 'The Farm' which can now be seen ahead – to the right of a hedge for the last part of the way. Go to the right of the farm, and onto a farm access road which leads to a metalled road. Turn left on this road to reach the 'major' road at Longnor. At present most of this route is blocked, and therefore choice 2 must be followed until it is cleared;

or

2. from the farm road at Bentley Ford Farm, turn left for 650 metres to meet a metalled road, and turn right on this to reach the 'major' road. Cross this road and take the road opposite, leading to the village of Longnor.

Longnor's name comes from *Longenalla* which is the old name for the Long Alder, which lines the Cound Brook on which the village lies. The building of Longnor Hall started in 1670, and St Mary's Church was b u i l t between 1 2 6 0 a n d 1 2 7 7 . The church has Oak box pews made by Richard Lee in 1723. The Moat house is 14th century.

To continue the walk. From the village centre turn right after the post office and school, and bend left when the road does. Follow the road until you reach a junction on the left, and turn along this road to reach the Old Forge and The Paper Mill which has been converted to a house. Cross over the Cound Brook by the footbridge provided and go through the gate on the right alongside the brook. Follow the brook

and go through another gate, then turn half-left to cross a small field and go through gate in left fence. Follow this line to go over the fence opposite, where a stile is missing. You are now in a large field. Cross direct with a wood some 50 metres to your right, widening to 100 metres from a right hedge at the far field end – yes, there is a stile, and a footbridge over a drainage ditch, hidden in the trees! Go over a further stile into a small field. Follow the right hedge to another over-grown double stile. Follow the right fence to cross a farm track and then, on the same line, head for a white painted stile giving access onto the railway embankment. Walk through Dogs Mercury (a dark green plant!) to reach the rail line. Cross the track with care (Shrewsbury to Ludlow line). Descend the far embankment through Bittersweet and Lesser Burdock, to reach another white stile. Turn right along a stream bank to walk through Pineappleweed (a plant with a strong pineapple smell when the head is crushed) with a wood to the right. Go through a gap between trees into a larger field, with the Cound Brook to the right. Follow the line of

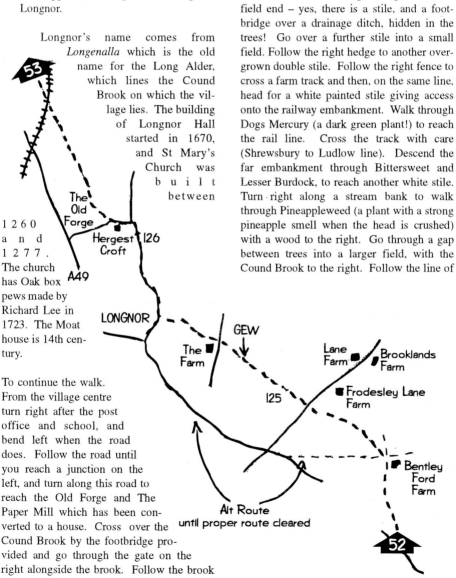

Scots Pine trees on the right across this field, then through a gap in trees into a smaller field. Walk on the right side of this field to the far side, then turn left along the fence/wall. Go over a stile and onto a house drive leading to the A49 road. Turn right for a short walk into Dorrington.

Dorrington has some buildings dating back to the 17th century. A big change to life came in 1853 when the Shrewsbury to Hereford railway line opened, with a station at Dorrington. Dick Whittington was not the only Lord mayor of London to come from the GEW route. John Boydell was born here in 1719, and became Lord Mayor in 1790.

Keep on the main A49 road as far as the crossroads, then turn left on the road signposted to Picklescott (Church Road). Pass the church of

St Edward, built in 1845. Just past the church you should be able to turn onto a path at Rowley's House on the right, then turn left at the back of the houses and go down a passage along the rear of the houses to reach 'The Maitlands' road. In 1996 the path is blocked, so until Shropshire County Council clear the problem carry on the road past the church to the end of the house row, then turn right onto 'The Maitlands'. Follow the road as it bears left on this new housing estate, and go to the left of No 33 along a passage way at the side of the house. When you are level with the back garden turn left over a double stile and footbridge.

Head diagonally right across the field and over a stile onto a minor road. Cross the road and continue on the same line (to the left of a hedge) aiming for a footbridge and stile 50 metres to the left of the field corner. Beyond this, aim across a large field directly for the left side of Corfield's Coppice Wood. When you reach a hedge line ***don't*** cross – keep on this side and turn left along the hedge. Follow the hedge now on your right until you pass the wood. The hedge then bears slightly right to a gate (and a path crossroad). Turn right here, follow the right hedge, then go through another gate, and head for a tree line and footbridge 50 metres from the right field corner (over a tributary of the Cound Brook).

The next field is again one where hedgerows have been taken out to create a larger field. Keep the hedge on the left until you reach a gate, with a stagnant stream to the left, and carry on to arrive at Cound Brook. In 1996 the footbridge was broken so you have the choice of risking the bridge, or fording the brook. Once over the brook turn half-left (ignore the farm track straight on), go through a gate and up the field to the left of a fence. The remains of a castle motte are to the left. Go over a stile onto the road at Stapleton.

Turn left to St John the Baptist church. The church is unique, having been built in the 12th and early-13th centuries with two storeys. In 1786 the two storeys were combined to leave the church with strange proportions. It also has some German candlesticks dating from 1500.

Take the road opposite the church. Lyth Hill is now very clear. Walk along the road for 750m until you reach a slight rise and a wood on the right. A footpath should now start up the banking on the left, so either climb up the bank and over the fence (or, if the stile is still missing, go 50 metres further on the road and over a gate on the left, then back up the field to the original point). Either way, once in the field there is a hedge to the left. Cross the field to a gate 50 metres to the right of the top left field corner. Through the gate carry on the same line to a gate onto the road, just left of the houses at Chatford hamlet.

Turn right on the road for 50 metres, then left before a farm barn. Go to the left of a fence at the rear of the farm and over a footbridge. Then, on the same line, go to left of a hedge aiming for the left side of Westley Farm on the road ahead. Once on the road turn left for 10 metres, then through a gate on the right between barns and through a gate at the rear of the farm. Go over to the left hedge and follow this to a gate. Cross the next field, following the line of electricity poles, and over a stile into a sparse wood at the base of Lyth Hill. Don't take the obvious track heading half-left, but climb straight up the hillside through two gates and turn right onto the stony road at the hilltop (or, if you

prefer, keep on the grass before the second gate and turn right parallel to the road). Either way, pass a number of houses on the left, one with the base of an old windmill which was built in 1835. On reaching the highest point there is a panoramic view point – the highest point of the hill is 169 metres.

The surrounding low land means that there are excellent views from Lyth Hill even though the hill is not very high. The Stiperstones and Earls Hill can be seen to the southwest, The Wrekin is to the east, Wenlock Edge and the hills of Brown Clee are to the southeast, and the environs of Shrewsbury can be seen to the northeast. There is a dearth of suitable paths to the east of Shrewsbury, and going west would be nice, but a long detour, therefore the GEW now goes north to the ancient city of Shrewsbury itself.

Continue along the stony track until a tarmac road joins from the right, and your own road becomes metalled. A further 100 metres brings you to a covered reservoir on the left. Turn left over a stile just past this reservoir. At the end of the reservoir fence now on your left enter a large field, and continue on the same line to cross the field. To the north, on your right, can be seen Grinshill – a small hill a long way on the other side of Shrewsbury. At the far side of the field carry on the same line, to the left of a fence. At the end of the second field turn half-right with the fence and go through

Lythwood farmyard. The path now becomes a tarmac road.

When you reach a house on the right, turn left through a stile into allotments, and turn right to be parallel to the road you have just left. Carry on into a small car park and out onto the road on the far side and into a housing estate (Lythwood road). Cross Glebe Road (staying on Lythwood Road), and pass The Beeches inn. There is a line of shops (post office, stores etc) on Lansdowne Road to your left. You are now in Bayston Hill.

The town of Bayston Hill was once more or less confined to the side of the A49 road to the east, but has spread over the years. There were once 12 inns along the A49 to serve the thirsty drovers – only three now remain. Lythwood Hall to the west of the town was designed by George Steuart, who was also the architect for the conversion of Tern Hall into the magnificent Attingham House in the late 18th century (a National Trust property 6km

to the east of Shrewsbury).

Carry on the road and take the next left, Castle Lane. At the end of the lane is a large house called 'The Castle'. Go along the path to the left of the house and into a field. Turn 30 degrees right to cross the field to a large Oak tree. Pulley Farm is now ahead, but bypass it by turning half-left at the tree, across a small field to a gate and then, with a hedge on your right, cross another small field to a minor road. Turn right for 150 metres, then go over a stile on the left and along the left fence to another minor road. Turn right on this road to cross the bridge over the busy A5 Shrewsbury bypass.

Continue on the road after crossing the A5 for a further 300 metres, then turn left over a stile and follow the stream on the right. The path crosses the stream and takes you to a large footbridge over Rea Brook. Follow a broad track through trees to Church Road, and turn right to pass a school before arriving at Holy

Chatford and Lyth Hill

Trinity church at Meole Brace.

Meole Brace was once a separate village, but has now become absorbed as a suburb of Shrewsbury. The old manor, Meole Hall, contains the site of the castle erected by the de Braceys in the 12th century, but which burnt down in 1669. The name Meole means "hill" or "sandy bank", and the Brace comes from the de Bracey family. The famous novelist Mary Webb was married in the church in 1912, and is buried in the cemetery. She wrote *The Golden Arrow* and *Gone to Earth*.

At the church turn left with the road until it meets Vicarage Road. Turn right on this for 150 metres, then left into Meole Walk. 50 metres on the right is a diagonal alley leading to a railway line (to Welshpool, Newtown, Machynlleth and Aberystwyth). Cross the line and turn half-right across a playing field to a point halfway along the far side, and up to the B4380 road. Turn left and cross the busy road to a footpath on the right side, about 100 metres from the roundabout. Turn down the footpath to the left side of the graveyard. This path arrives at another minor road. Turn right for 20 metres, then left down a tarmaced path to a valley and cross the Rad Brook. Once over the brook climb back uphill. The track soon branches – take the right fork (known as Beehive Lane), and arrive at Kingsland Road.

Cross over, and slightly left, to go down a toll road to Kingsland Bridge over the river Severn. Don't worry, cars are charged but pedestrians are free! The River Severn has

not been seen on the GEW for many miles. Although now much further inland, the river is still mighty. Just past the toll booth you reach a main road (Town Walls). Don't cross the road but turn right immediately – back on yourself – down a small lane to the riverside. Turn left. There is now a long walk along the riverside. At numerous points you can break off to enter the city.

Shrewsbury is the county town and is the natural centre of the region. The city was founded by the Romans in the 5th century, and is on a rocky spur in an oxbow meander above the River Severn. In the confusion which seemed to reign after the withdrawal of the Romans, the city became the seat of the princes of Powys from the fifth to the eighth centuries.

Roger de Montgomery built the castle shortly after the conquest to secure the border lands. This would have been built of wood initially, but was rebuilt in stone in the 12th century and fell into disrepair in the 14th century. The last time any action took place was during the Civil War, when a small Parliamentary force captured the castle and town with little bloodshed. Thomas Telford made alterations after 1780 both inside and outside. The castle is near the ornate railway station, and is now the home of the Shropshire Regimental museum which houses many displays telling the story of the Regiment's history. The castle is open to the public from Tuesday to Saturday every week.

The famous Battle of Shrewsbury was fought at Battlefield, to the north of the city, in 1403. Hotspur (Sir Henry Percy, son of the Earl of

Northumberland) lost the battle and was hung, drawn and quartered in the city immediately after the battle.

The city is rich in old houses, with many fine examples of black and white houses from the 15th, 16th and 17th centuries. It is said by many to be the finest Tudor town in England. The civic library is 17th century. St Mary's Church is 12th to 17th century, and St Chad's is one of England's few classical round churches – it was rebuilt in 1790 after the previous church collapsed. There is also a house where John Wesley preached. The Benedictine Abbey of St Peter and St Paul was founded by Roger de Montgomery in 1083.

Each year the city holds the popular Shrewsbury flower show, which attracts many thousands of visitors.

George Farquhar wrote *The Recruiting Officer* play here in 1705. William Hazlitt bought a copy of Milton's *Paradise Lost* here, and his first 'publication' was a letter to the Shrewsbury Chronicle in 1791. Poet John Hamilton Reynolds was born in the city in 1794.

GR SJ 488 121

SHREWSBURY

River Severn

Kingsland Bridge

KINGSLAND

136

B4380

135

MEOLE + BRACE

FB

56

The city's most famous son is Charles Robert Darwin who was born at The Mount in 1809, and in 1818 was a boarder at Shrewsbury school (now the library). His mother was the eldest daughter of Josiah Wedgwood, who had founded his pottery in Etruria, Stoke-on-Trent. There is a statue of Darwin outside the library. He is famous for his voyage as a naturalist on HMS Beagle from 1831 to 1836, and his subsequent book *On the Origin of Species by Means of Natural Selection* which was published in 1859. He also wrote *The Descent of Man*. He died in 1882 and is buried in Westminster Abbey.

Other famous pupils at Shrewsbury School were Sir Philip Sydney, Frederick William Faber (who wrote the hymns *My God, how wonderful thou art*, and *Pilgrims of the night*) and Samual Butler, author of *Erewhon*.

Robert Clive was born in Market Drayton in 1725. Better known as Clive of India, he established British rule in the sub-continent. On his return he became a mayor of Shrewsbury and also an MP before his early death in 1774.

The city's even more famous 'son' is brother Cadfael, the fictional hero of Ellis Peters' (whose real name was Edith Pargeter). Cadfael was a medieval detective monk living in Shrewsbury Abbey.

TEN
Shrewsbury - Wem
(17.25 miles or 27.6 km)

From Kingsland Bridge keep alongside the river to pass first under Greyfriars pedestrian bridge, then English Bridge with its stone shell motifs. The bridge is lined with hanging baskets in summer. The riverside walk is very pleasant, with the occasional passing boat carrying tourists. There are numerous places to break off for further visits into the city. The next bridge is the one carrying the railway tracks into the station – alas it is functional, but not pretty. Beyond this bridge is another pedestrian one, then a weir, and then a long walk to the A5112 road bridge. The city environs have now begun to give way to country again. The riverside walk has given way to a small road, and then to just a foot-path. Once you have passed the A5112 bridge still carry on north along the river bank until the river begins to make an obvious right bend. At this point the path splits, go uphill away from the river, but don't go up as far as the road – when a transverse path is reached turn right.

The river appears for a short time again, down to your right, as you walk through this green oasis to the northeast of the city. The track now begins to widen, and there are some remains of the old Shrewsbury Canal on your left.

Continue on the wide track until you arrive at

English Bridge at Shrewsbury

the metalled road going across the path to
serve Pimley Manor. Cross the road and
carry on the track to take the new underpass
of the A49. Follow the track as it bears right.
The old dry canal is to the right, and the path
is now on the canal towpath. The canal used
to run from Uffington to Castlefields in
Shrewsbury, and was used to transport coal.
Houses can be seen across fields to the left,
and the A49 bridge over the Severn is to the
right. At this point there is a stile to the right
which should be crossed into a field. Go
over the field diagonally left and onto a
house patio. This is a poignant moment,
being the last glimpse of the River
Severn.

Cross the patio and pick up
an old track which
brings you out at

the side of Holy Trinity
church in Uffington vil-
lage.

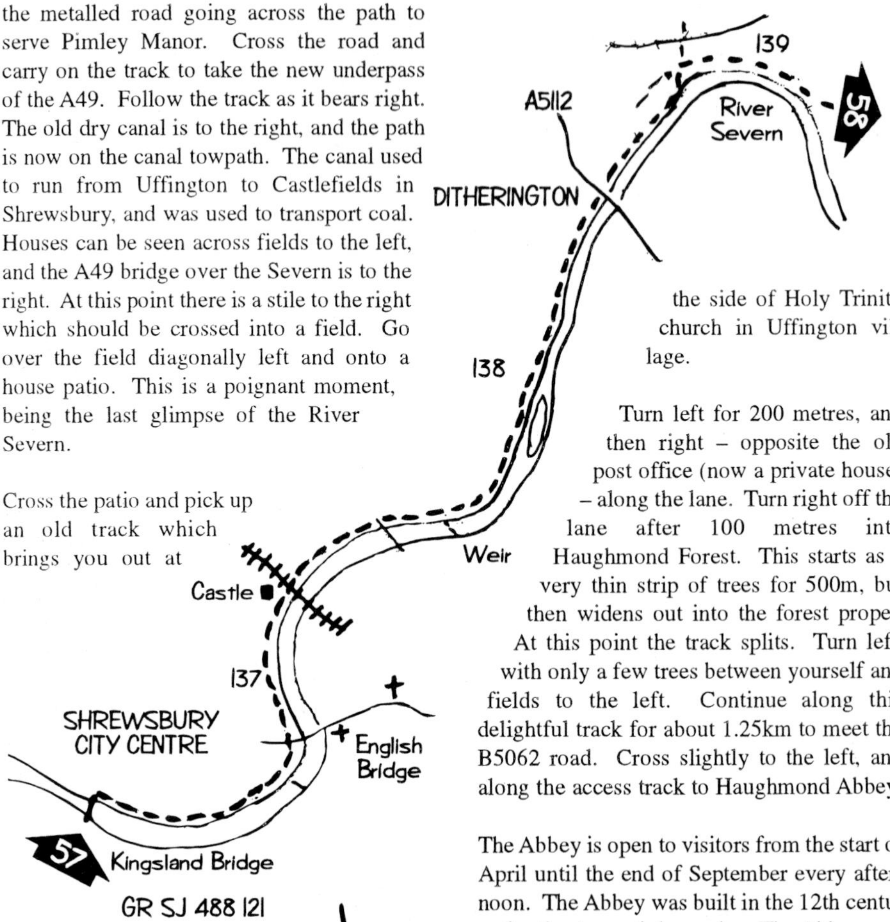

Turn left for 200 metres, and
then right – opposite the old
post office (now a private house)
– along the lane. Turn right off the
lane after 100 metres into
Haughmond Forest. This starts as a
very thin strip of trees for 500m, but
then widens out into the forest proper.
At this point the track splits. Turn left,
with only a few trees between yourself and
fields to the left. Continue along this
delightful track for about 1.25km to meet the
B5062 road. Cross slightly to the left, and
along the access track to Haughmond Abbey.

The Abbey is open to visitors from the start of
April until the end of September every after-
noon. The Abbey was built in the 12th century for the Augustinian order. The Abbey was
one of those demolished by order of

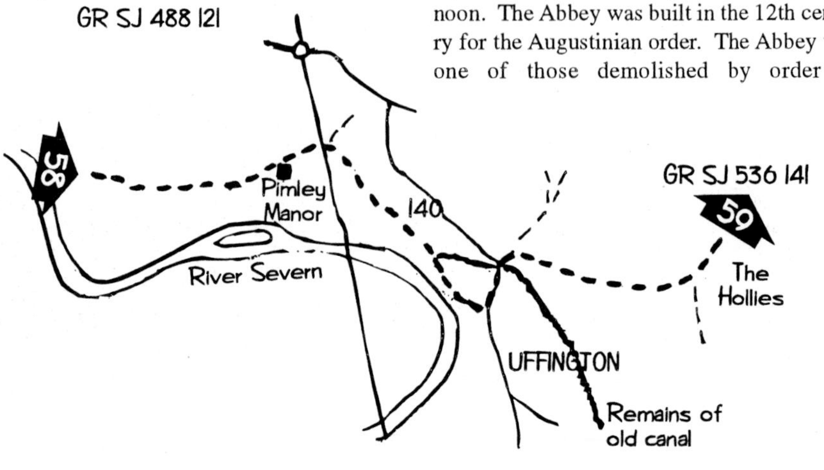

Henry VIII, but there are extensive remains to be visited. The site is now cared for by English Heritage.

The paths in this area have been altered since the last OS map was produced. Go over a stile to the west (left) of the Abbey, and round to the north of the Abbey (with excellent views of the ruins), to reach a track. Go straight across the track, up a slight rise, and over a stile. Head directly across the field to a stile onto the road, and then immediately double back on yourself to go along the drive to Haughmond Farm. Go to the left of the farm buildings, through gates to the back of the farm, and then straight out onto a clear farm track. When the top of the track is reached there is a good view of Grinshill ahead. Ebury Hill is to the right rising to 105 metres, with its obligatory ancient Briton hill fort.

Turn left, and follow the left fence to a gate. Then turn half-right to cross the field to the distant left corner. New Coppice Wood is to the left. Once you have reached the field corner don't cross the stile, but turn right in the field and complete another field side (with

Colins Rough Wood now to the left). On this leg you can cut across part of the field as it recedes for a time on the left, and head for the far corner.

Go over a stile and continue on this line, with a hedge to the left. Follow the hedge as it bears gently left. Go over a stile into a large field. Head straight across it on a line marked by a course of trees, and aim for the right of the buildings of Wheatley Farm. Exit the farm by the track on the far side, which goes over a small tributary of the Severn, and follow the track as it bends around, until it suddenly ends at a field entrance. Go through a gate on the left, and follow the right hedge to the A53 road.

The Dog in the Lane inn is opposite – very handy for refreshment. Cross the road and go along the lane to the left side of the inn, for the walk through Upper Astley and on to the village of Astley with St Mary's church. Follow Astley Lane northwards all the way to Hadnall village. This is a long way on the lane, but is pretty and little used by vehicles. Pass through the small village to arrive at the A49 road. Cross over onto a minor road

Haughmond Abbey

(Wood Road). Go past the bowling green, and then turn right after a further 20 metres..to a kissing gate and into a field (opposite Willow Court).

Part way through the field is the remains of a moat from the old Hadnall Hall which has been long demolished. The hall was the hiding place for the two princes, Edward and Richard, who ended up dying in the Tower of London in 1483. General Viscount Rowland Hill was born near here at Prees Hall. He fought in the Peninsular and at Waterloo in the Napoleonic wars, and is buried in Hadnall church. There is a column statue to Hill in Shrewsbury – the column stands 40.66 metres tall and is surmounted by a 5.2 metre statue.

Pass out of the field by another kissing gate onto a track, with the church of St Mary Magdelene to the right. Turn left for 10 metres, then right over a stile and pass Church Farm. Cross a field and go to the left of a small pool at the far field side, and then directly across a field centre 100 metres from the right hedge. Enter a green lane and then a house drive, and turn right to Ladymas Lane at Providence Grove. Cross the lane, keeping on the same line, through more kissing gates, and into a narrow green defile. You reach an old brick wall. Here the path splits. The right fork goes to the A49 road, so go left and gradually away from the busy road. When you finally leave this defile and enter a field, keep 30 metres right of a hedge. Go over a stile, follow the left hedge, and exit onto the unmade Mill Lane.

Turn right for 10 metres, then left, to continue behind a cottage and an old converted windmill. There is plenty of Ground Ivy underfoot. Leave the wood and enter a field. Walk across the centre guided by a solitary

GR SJ 532 180

Oak tree. You are now in the Hardwicke estate. Go over a stile and turn half-left, before going over another stile into another wood. Keep in the right side of the wood to pass Hardwicke stables and reach a minor road. Turn left for 100 metres, then leave the road at a gate on the right and head towards Grinshill, with New Plantation wood on the left at one point. At the far end of the plantation go through a gate, and across a field aiming for the far right

A53

Wheatley Farm

144

Colin's Rough

New Coppice

143

Ebury Hill Fort

Haughmond Farm

142

Haughmond Abbey

B5062

141   Haughmond Hill

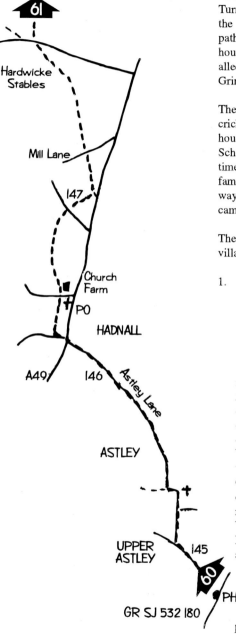

side, along a field edge and onto a minor road. Turn right for five metres, then over a stile on the left to continue on the same line. This path leads half-right into the back garden of a house, then to a short green lane onto the metalled Sandy Lane. Turn left on the lane to Grinshill.

The Jacobean stone grange, overlooking the cricket pitch and known locally as the 'pest' house, was built in 1617 for Shrewsbury School as a country refuge from the city in times of plague. The Grinshill quarry is famous for its stone. The stone for the doorway of No 10 Downing Street in London came from the quarry.

There is a choice of routes from here to the village of Clive to the north —

1. from Sandy Lane turn right for 20 metres, then left on a track to pass All Saints Church which was built of local red sandstone in 1839. This ancient track curves left uphill, and then past a house to reach a metalled road. Turn right and pass the beautiful All Saints Church at Clive, with its white sandstone spire. The church is mainly 1885-94, but with a medieval core. There are beautiful windows depicting male saints, and female figures carved from wood holding up the roof. Walk down Drawwell (a road) to reach the 'major road' in Clive centre, passing Clive Hall which was built in the 14th century. It has a timber frame and herringbone brick, and was the birthplace of William Wycherley in 1640. He wrote the Restoration comedies *The Country Wife* and *The Plain Dealer.*

or

2. from Sandy Lane turn right and pass the Elephant and Castle inn. Continue along this road for a further 600 metres, where there is a path going uphill

on the left. The whole of the top of Grinshill is quite wooded, and there is a nature trail laid out. The car park is on the northeast side of the hill. A leaflet is available that takes you around nine points of interest – going up the path starts you off at point 8! There is a rock

GR SJ 518 251

house dated 1790. The trail leads up a long incline, down which stone used to be brought from Bridge quarry. The keystone for English Bridge in Shrewsbury was brought down this way – the wagon carrying the 10.5 ton stone being drawn by 12 Shire horses in 1773. At the top of the incline is a panorama looking south to give views of The Wrekin to the Welsh hills. Carrying on the same line as the incline brings you to the heart of the bridge quarry, which was worked from Roman days up to the 1960s. This was the home of the fossil reptile Rhynchosaur.

Strike off on the path going northwest, and when the path splits keep to the wooded side to drop down to the minor road just north of All Saints Church at Clive. Turn right to walk down Drawwell to reach Clive centre.

Whichever route you choose, you arrive at the 'main road' in Clive. Most of the houses are built of local Grinshill stone, in shades of grey, honey and red. Copper mine tunnels extend under the village. The mine was worked from Roman times until 1886.

Turn right, then left onto Wem Road. Walk north along the road for approximately 400 metres, then turn right on a metalled farm access road. The metal peters out after 400 metres at Clive Wood Farm. Just after the farm the track splits – take the left track. After 300 metres a path comes in, over a stile from the right. Carry on for a further 200 metres, and go over the stile on the left to follow the right side of a hedge for two long fields, then the path changes to the left hedge side for one field. After this turn 30 degrees left until you are level with Trench Hall School, then turn half-right (north) to cross the centre of this field and finally arrive at a metalled lane at Tilley Green. Go straight

Astley Church

Grinshill

Patches Farm

Hanley Child

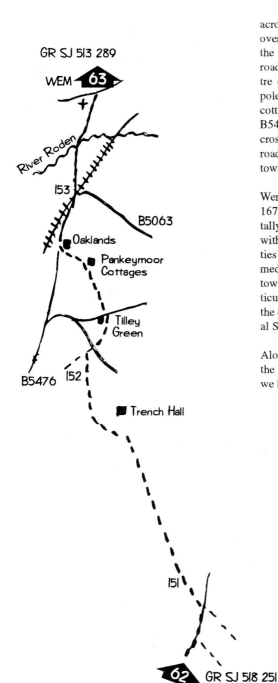

GR SJ 513 289

WEM 63

River Roden

153

B5063

Oaklands

Pankeymoor Cottages

Tilley Green

B5476 152

Trench Hall

151

62 GR SJ 518 251

across the lane and onto a green track, then over a stile and turn 30 degrees left to walk to the rear of a house and onto another minor road. Cross the road and cross the field centre opposite, guided by a line of electricity poles, to arrive at the left side of Pankeymoor cottages. Follow the track left to reach the B5476 road. Turn right along the road and cross under the railway bridge. Follow the road, and across the River Roden, into Wem town centre.

Wem started life as a Saxon settlement. In 1677 a 14 year old girl, Jane Churm, accidentally set the thatch roof of her home alight with a candle – which resulted in 140 properties burning down. As a result there are few medieval properties left in the town. The town was the home of Henry Eckford, an horticulturalist who developed the sweet pea at the end of the 19th century. There is an annual Sweet Pea show.

Along the walk you have already encountered the birthplace of two Lord Mayors, and now we have a third – Thomas Adams was born in

Elephant and Castle, Grinshill

The Castle Inn, Wem

the town in 1586 and became Lord Mayor of London in the mid-1600s. Judge George Jeffreys was noted for brutality. He was made Lord Chancellor in 1685, and also became the first Baron of Wem in the same year. He fittingly died in the tower of London in 1689. William Hazlitt lived here for most of his early formative years.

ELEVEN
Wem - Malpas
(17.75 miles or 28.4 km)

On entering Wem turn right on the High Street, then left on New Street and continue until it changes to Whitchurch Road. Turn left, just after the graveyard, into Love Lane. This is where couples from Wem would do their courting in olden days, and probably still do!

The lane soon becomes an unmetalled farm track. Leave the track and enter a field. Cross a stile on the right, halfway through the field. Over this stile turn half-left to the far corner. A stile and footbridge take you onto a narrow track, and via stables to a road at Creamore Bank. Turn left on the road (signposted to Edstaston), until you reach a road junction to the left at Ryebank. Opposite this junction turn right over a stile. Keep the hedge to the left in the first field, then over a stile head 30 degrees left across the next field – and the corner of the next. Turn half-right over a stile to head for Edstaston House, cross one field, then over a stile half-left (and to the right of a small stand of shrubs in the field centre). You are now heading well to the left of the house, before arriving at the road at St Mary the Virgin Church in Edstaston, an early Norman chapel built in 1150. The war memorial here tells the story of many villages – from this one small village 13 men were killed in the First World War, and three in the Second World War.

Turn left, and soon pass over the line of an old canal which has now disappeared – this was

St Mary the Virgin Church, Edstaston

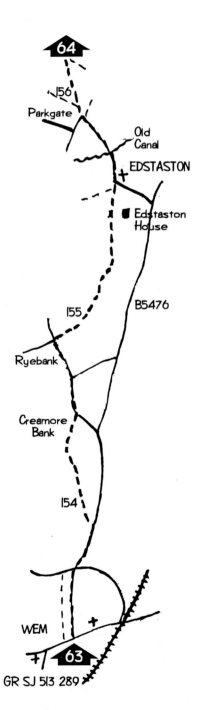

the Prees branch of the Ellesmere canal, itself a branch of the Shropshire Union Llangollen branch canal. Follow the road until it turns sharp left. The footpath goes to the right and then immediately left on a farm track for 100 metres. Turn right with the track for 50 metres, then off on the left into a field. Cross half-right. At the far field side go on to the left side of a hedge. Eventually a stile appears off to your left. At this point cut away from the hedge and head directly for the stile. It is at times like this, in the vastness of large fields, that you can be forgiven for wondering just where you are in England! *Nil Desperandum*, just head for that stile, with a small pond to its right (Rose Farm buildings are across two small fields to the left). Pass a second pool on the left, and then proceed along the left hedge and onto a track leading to a minor road. Turn right. The lane becomes Green Lane and then, when another lane joins from the right, it becomes Gilbert's Lane. Carry on to reach a T-junction at Whixall, a spread out village with no obvious centre.

Cross the road and onto a Nettle infested green lane to reach Church Farm. Over a stile go ahead half-left to cross a field, and pass to the right of a clump of trees and a pond. Go over two more stiles, then aim 30 degrees left to a stile at the far field side. This part of the walk has been in company with the Shropshire Way which now turns right. The GEW carries on – aim 30 degrees right towards the houses of Welsh End ahead. Go across the field centre to reach a hedge line, with a drainage ditch on the far side. Turn half-right here in this field, and head for the far left corner. The stile is 100 metres short of the field corner. Go over the stile and a footbridge, and diagonally across the field – a chapel and graveyard are over to the left on the roadside. Cross another footbridge and a field to a small lane. Turn left to the main road at Welsh End village.

River Teme at Knightwick

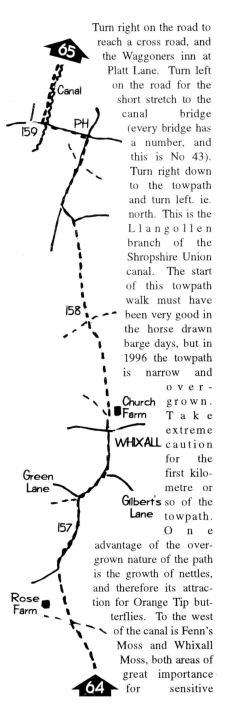

Turn right on the road to reach a cross road, and the Waggoners inn at Platt Lane. Turn left on the road for the short stretch to the canal bridge (every bridge has a number, and this is No 43). Turn right down to the towpath and turn left. ie. north. This is the Llangollen branch of the Shropshire Union canal. The start of this towpath walk must have been very good in the horse drawn barge days, but in 1996 the towpath is narrow and over-grown. Take extreme caution for the first kilo-metre or so of the towpath. One advantage of the over-grown nature of the path is the growth of nettles, and therefore its attrac-tion for Orange Tip but-terflies. To the west of the canal is Fenn's Moss and Whixall Moss, both areas of great importance for sensitive species of plants. This is a very beautiful walk along the tow-path. The cantilever bridge at Brickwalls is the first crossing point to be reached and is a per-fect example of canal engineering. Next, go under a brick bridge giving field access to Springhill farm. Carry on to the next bridge (No 40) known as Blackoe bridge, and then the disused railway bridge (No 39). The railway bridge used to carry the line from Whitchurch to Oswestry (typical times were leav-ing Whitchurch at 0817, Fenn's Bank 0823, Bettisfield 0831, Welshampton 0834, Ellesmere 0843, Frankton 0 8 4 8 , Whittington 0856, and arriv-ing at Oswestry at 0900). Pass under another field access bridge (No 38). Crosswort, with its lovely clustered yellow flowers, is grow-ing along the canal bank. The next bridge (No 37) is unique on British canals, having a 'built in cupboard' in the right support, which goes through to a similar door on the far side.

This is a long canal section, but exceedingly beautiful, and there is also an occasional pleasure boat passing on this very popular Llangollen canal. There are only four other *short* canal side paths after this en-route to Berwick.

The Welsh border is approximately 350 metres west of this point.

The next bridge (No 36) at Blackoe cottages would be an ideal place to leave the canal onto a path going north, but has no official exit point. Therefore carry on the towpath to reach bridge No 35, another cantilever bridge.

There are now two options on the GEW —

1. leave the canal here by going through the gate on the left of the bridge, onto a farm track, and bearing round with it to the right to reach the A525 road. Cross the road and go to the left of Hadley Pool, then turn right to head towards Hadley Farm. Once you reach the farm buildings turn left in the farmyard and go over the stile at the back of the farm. Head across a field, but slightly left, down into a small valley and cross the footbridge over Red Brook.

Climb the 'hill' on the other side, and then follow the left of a hedge. The hedge becomes a fence, then when it changes to a hedge again turn right with it, going over stiles but keeping to the left of the hedge. Pass 200 metres to the right of Bubney Farm, and then join the track from the farm to follow it to the A41 road. Turn left on the road, and walk to the junction of the A41 and B5395 roads where there is the Horse and Jockey inn.

WHITCHURCH CENTRE

This is the hamlet of Grindley Brook. Cross the road and go along the track to the left side of the petrol station to the canal. Don't cross, but turn left on the towpath. This option takes 3.7km off the route;

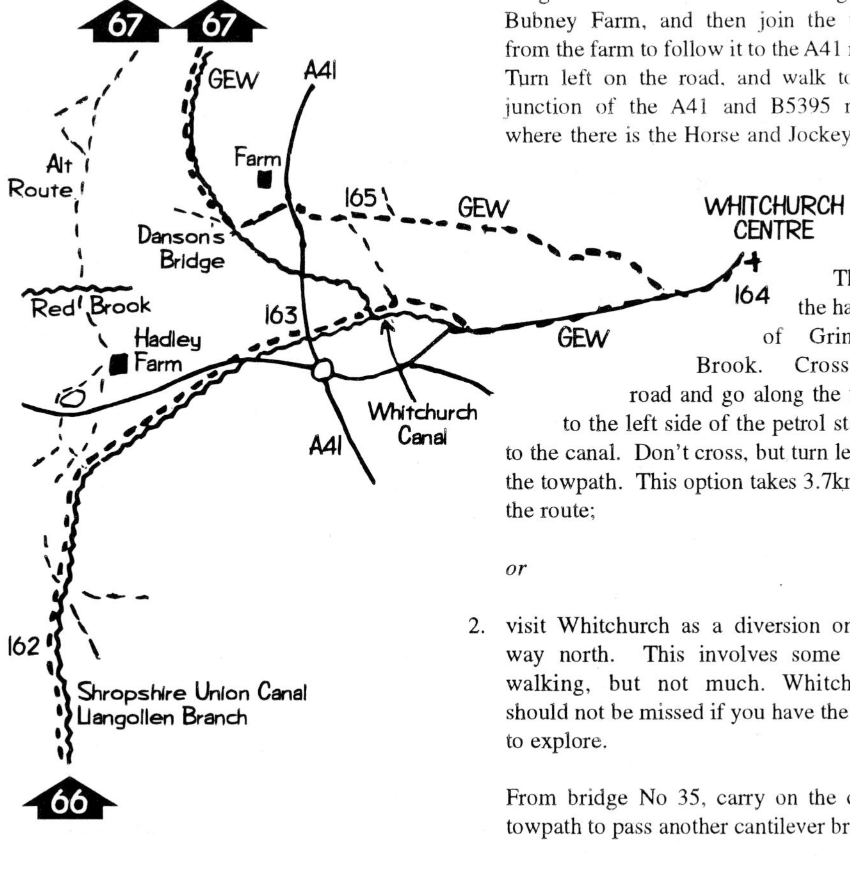

or

2. visit Whitchurch as a diversion on the way north. This involves some road walking, but not much. Whitchurch should not be missed if you have the time to explore.

From bridge No 35, carry on the canal towpath to pass another cantilever bridge,

Kyre Brook at Tenbury Wells

Church Stretton from Three Fingers Rock

and then go under the A525 Wrexham road. Immediately after this bridge, on the right bank (and therefore no access) is Viking Afloat camping and boat hire company. Carry on the towpath to go under the new bridge carrying the A41 bypass road. You shortly arrive at another cantilever bridge – this one is called New Mills Bridge. Cross the bridge – hopefully it has been left down by the last boat to pass, but if not there will be another boat along shortly and they can lower the cantilever. You are now on the Whitchurch branch canal. The canal branch was built in 1811, abandoned in 1944, and unfortunately filled in the 1950s. The line of the canal is now built upon, but the first short section of 200 metres was reopened in October 1993 (and there are hopes to open a rerouted canal all the way to Whitchurch in the future). You can either leave the canal via a gate on the left after 100 metres and then walk on a track past stables and a small canal shop to reach a bridge, or walk along the 200 metres of towpath and then climb up a flight of steps just before the blocked-up bridge.

Either way go across the bridge to Chemistry Road. Turn left on the road, which soon changes name to Smallbrook Road. Keep following this line as the name changes again to Sherrymill Hill and then Yardington to arrive at High Street, and St Alkmund's Church.

The Romans built a camp in Whitchurch as a stop over point between Chester and Wroxeter. The Roman camp was called *Mediolanum,* meaning "the place in the middle of the plain".

The first church was possibly built in the early 900s by Ethelfreda, the Queen of Mercia, and named after St Alkmund – a Northumbrian prince who was killed in the battle of Worcester in 822. Alkmund was the younger son of King Alcred of Northumbria. This church was replaced by one built by William de Warren after the Norman conquest, which in turn was replaced again, probably in the 14th century. The church you see today was built in 1712/13 and is said to have been influenced by Sir Christopher Wren's building of St Paul's in London.

The town of Whitchurch is known for its tower clocks, and Thomas Joyce of Whitchurch built the church clock in 1849. The company was established in 1690 and turret clocks are still manufactured in the town to this day.

Font at St Alkmunds Church, Whitchurch

Bridge 37, Shropshire Union Canal

John Talbot is one of the town's famous sons. He fought Owain Glyndawr, and was then made Lord Lieutenant of Ireland. He died, at the age of seventy, in the battle of Castillon in 1453 which was the final battle of the Hundred Years War against France. His heart is buried in the church porch, and his bones in the Talbot tomb inside the church. The iron tombstones in the graveyard are worthy of note, dating from 1798 to 1865.

Randolph Caldecott was born in Chester in 1846, but worked in Whitchurch from 1861 to 1867. He died at the young age of 40, but made a name for himself as an illustrator of books – *The house that Jack Built* and *John Gilpin* – and artistic correspondent for the *London Society, Harpers & Daily Graphic* in the USA. His oil paintings were exhibited at the Royal Academy.

Probably the most famous name in

Whitchurch is German Edward Jones, born in the town in 1862. Fairly early in his career he changed his name to Edward German. He left home in 1880 to study at Shrewsbury, and later the Royal Academy in London. He is not as famous as Elgar, but he composed a number of famous works – *The Emerald Isle, Merrie England, The Princess of Kensington, Tom Jones* and *Fallen Fairies*. He also composed music for Rudyard Kipling's *Just So Stories*. King George V gave him a knighthood in 1928. He died in 1936 and was buried in the graveyard in Whitchurch. He said of himself —

Melodically, I may be a success,
Harmonically, I may be respectable,
Orchestrally, I may be sound,
Socially, I am a mistake.

There are a number of shops in the high street worthy of a visit, but when you have had enough, retrace your steps as far as the dip in the road where the canal used to run under the road. Just before the dip, and before Waterside Close, there is a postbox and path on the right. Go down the steps and bend left to houses and a path fork. Take the path left to an estate road. Cross and take the path going off at the right side, through fields and a wood's edge into another field. Bear right up a slight rise to a new housing estate. Keep to the right of the houses and gardens on a path which bears away, and over a footbridge and stile into another field. Cross half-right and into a small green lane, with Birch trees to the right and Hawthorn trees to the left. These soon end and you go over a stile to emerge into another field. Go directly across this field and over a stile, then half-left across another field to end up 50 metres to the right of the left corner. Cross a footbridge and stile then go directly across the next field to a gap and stile in a hedge. At this point there is a sign for two paths – one goes right but the GEW goes half-right across the field to another footbridge and stile. Over this turn left for 70 metres then, as the hedge bears left, carry on the same line across the field to a stile alongside a gate. Turn half-right and cross the field to a stile leading down to the A41 bypass road. You may be lucky to find Bittersweet growing in this area.

Cross the road and go on the concrete drive opposite leading to the abandoned Danson's Farm. After 50 metres turn left over a stile to follow the left side of a hedge for 150 metres to Danson's Bridge. Cross the bridge (No 30), go right over two stiles down to the towpath and turn left on the narrow and crumbling towpath. The path improves after about 500 metres. You finally arrive at moorings and then locks. This is the Grindley Brook flight of locks. After the third lock follow the towpath under the A41 road, and pass more locks to arrive at a sign pointing the way left to the Horse and Jockey inn. Shortly after this is the footbridge at the end of option 1.

Here is the hamlet of Grindley Brook. Apart from the flight of locks, its main claim to fame is that it is the end of the northern extension of the Shropshire Way, and also the start of the Sandstone Trail (which goes from here to Frodsham).

You soon reach the tunnel under the disused railway line (this ran from a junction east of Chester, via Tattenhall, Malpas and on to Whitchurch. The train used to take 32 minutes from Chester to Malpas, with a further 12 minutes to Whitchurch). You have now entered the county of Cheshire. When Shires were created about AD 900 this county received the name of *Legeceaster scir*, which later became *Cestre shire*, and then *Chestershire*, and finally Cheshire. Cheshire is known for its cheese. There are three kinds of Cheshire cheese – the crumbly white, its red dyed counterpart, and the connoisseurs' blue.

Carry on the towpath for a further 600 metres to Jackson's Bridge (No 26). Go under the bridge and turn left. Once in the field aim for a stile in the far right corner. Carry on the same line in the next field and onto a minor road. Cross the road and into fields, again keeping on the same line, with a hedge to the right through two fields. The countryside has now changed from the flatness of North Shropshire to 'rolling' country. Leave the hedge/stream on your right to go over a stile, and follow the left hedge to the A41 road.

Turn right for 100 metres, then left off the road onto a path and into the orchard behind 'The Riddings' house. The orchard becomes a field. Head towards the right side of High Ash Farm and onto its tarmac drive. Go straight across to the left corner of a small field. Turn left over a stile hidden behind a wooden shed, and enter a large field beyond the farm. At the next gate a bridleway sign goes left and right, but the GEW carries straight on to follow the right hedge for two more fields, and then goes through a gate on the right (just after a small pond). The dis-

St Oswalds Church, Malpas

Three Fingers Rock and Caer Caradoc

Cantilever Bridge at Brickwalls

Malpas Cottages

used Chester to Whitchurch railway line is now down to the left. Carry on alongside the line for 200 metres, and then turn left under a bridge on the old line.

Turn right for 50 metres, then left to a gate into the rear of a farm. Turn right here on the farm access track, which soon draws alongside the old railway line again at Bradley Green. Don't climb up to the road at the bridge, but follow the farm track as it bends left to join a road. Follow this minor road to the junction with the B5395.

Turn right for 200 metres to the entrance to Bradley Hall. Go over a stile just to the left of the farm drive, and head half-right to a stile at the far field hedge (about 100 metres left of the farm buildings). From this point go half-right again through the next field, to the far corner, then turn left to climb to the right of the hedge. At the top of the climb the hedge turns left. You should go ahead, but slightly

left to a stile, then directly ahead to cut off the corner of the hedge to the right. Then leave the hedge to go straight ahead to a gate onto a track. Turn left and follow the track, which soon becomes metalled, to arrive at the cottages at Bradley Brook.

Follow the road as it goes downhill for 200 metres and then turns left over a brook. Carry on the road for a further 150 metres until the road turns right, then after a further 150 metres turn left through a gate. Head 30 degrees to the right to a tree corner on the far field side, and follow a short hedge on the left into another field. Follow the right hedge/fence until it meets a farm track. Turn right on this for 150 metres, then leave it to follow the left fence. When this ends carry on the same line as closely as possible (heading towards the church). Go through gates and arrive at a brick wall (the back of a line of garages). Go over a stile through the garages and houses, and onto Springfield Avenue.

Turn left and follow the avenue around to the right. Turn left at the road junction onto Springfield Road. Turn right on the B5395 into Malpas centre.

The Romans made a camp in the area. After the Norman conquest Hugh Lupus was made Earl of Chester, and his son Fitz Hugh the Baron of Malpas. The town's position, near the Welsh border, made it of strategic importance, and it was made part of the defence castle area including Skocklach and Oldcastle.

Here is a tale to whet your appetite and thirst. A notice in the Red Lion inn informs visitors —

'King James Ist, travelling incognito, stopped at what is now the Red Lion inn. The house was frequented in the evening by the rector and curate of the parish. The King joined in the conversation. When the company were about to separate the curate proposed that the stranger be given some mark of hospitality – so that he should be exempt from paying any part of the evenings expenses.

All the company agreed, except the rector, who insisted that every tub should stand upon its own staves: with several other expressions that convinced the monarch that there were better rectors in the Kingdom than the one in Malpas. And, laying by his disguise, he pronounced to them that he was their King, and that from henceforth the curate should also be a rector, and enjoy the same privileges and emoluments'.

The chair in which the monarch sat was preserved, and to this day is in the hall of the inn. The Red Lion façade was built in the 1920s, but the inn was built as an ale house in the 12th century.

St Oswald's Church is one of the finest in the county and is dedicated to Oswald, King of Northumbria, killed in battle against Penda, the heathen King of Mercia. The battle took place in 642 at Maserfield (possibly where Oswestry now stands). The date of the first church is not known, but the present church was built in the 14th century. The church is very beautiful. It contains a 13th century iron bound chest, a 15th century font and also some pews from 1680.

Bishop Heber was born here in 1775. His father was rector from 1770 to 1804. The Bishop wrote many hymns. *Holy, Holy, Holy, Lord God Almighty, Bread of the world in mercy broken,* and *From Greenland's icy mountain are amongst them.*

There is some beautiful furniture and ceilings, the 15th century nave roof is of the camber – beam type and is enriched with gilded bosses, angels, and crows feet. There are tombs to Sir Hugh Cholmondeley (pronounced "Chumly") and his wife Mary, and Sir Randal and Lady Brereton.

The castle remains are to the north of the church. The Motte dominates the churchyard, but there are no traces of a Bailey.

MALPAS
PO
GR SJ 488 473
|7|
|70
Bradley Brook
Disused Railway
Bradley Hall
69

TWELVE
Malpas - Tarporley
(15.25 miles or 24.4 km)

From the Red Lion inn turn right along Well Street. When it joins another road (with a post box and telephone kiosk), bear left, then immediately left again on a small lane for 250 metres. Another lane joins from the left, with a house at the junction. Go to the left of the house, through a gate into a field, and then cross it half-left. Aim for the far left corner, and then turn right on a farm track. Carry on the same line onto a footpath, with a hedge to the right for one field – then cross a farm track, and go over a stile to swop to the right of a hedge. At the end of this field you meet a path going left and right – turn right within the field, then go over a stile at the end and turn left along the hedge. Keep the hedge, and ponds, to the left as you pass Ebnal Farm and go onto a minor road. Cross the road. Bickerton Hill is now very evident to the northeast.

Follow the track to the left of a line of Hawthorn bushes, to meet the old Chester to Whitchurch railway line again. Turn left on the trackbed for 400 metres (through gates) to reach a stile, then turn half-right through two fields to Cholmondeley Road. Turn right on the road, and cross the busy A41 road. There is now a very pleasant 1.25 km walk on the quiet road. First you pass some of the houses of Hampton Heath on the left, then the minor road to Hampton House on the left, to reach a cross road at Hampton Post. Carry on across the road (the road you are walking has now changed name to Shay Lane). From the crossroads walk a further 400 metres (but *don't miss* the triangulation point in the right hedge at the roadside at 133 metres), then turn left off the road and onto a path with the hedge to your right. You are now heading downhill towards Manor House Farm.

Hampton House

Hampton Post

Hampton Heath

173

A41

Disused Railway

EBNAL

Ebnal Farm

172

B5069

MALPAS

B5069

GR SJ 488 473   B5395

Malpas Market Cross

Bickerton Hill is straight ahead, with Peckforton Hill stretching off to your right. These are the first hills since Grinshill, and stretch for some 7km. History tells us that Cheshire used to be a large inland sea, hence the *'wich'* towns where the salt collected underground when the sea dried out. From here it seems obvious that Bickerton and Peckforton would have been islands in that sea a million years ago.

100 metres before you reach the farm the path has now been diverted – turn right over a stile onto a pre-1948 path route. Pass a pool on your right, then go over a stile and turn to follow the left hedge on a detour around the farm. There is a large pool to the left, and then the path changes to the left side of a hedge and fence. Regain a northerly direction by turning right over stiles, following a fence on the right. Just before you reach a house turn right to follow another fence and exit onto a minor road. Cross the road and follow the Sandstone Trail signpost on the metalled access road to Larkton Hall. 100 metres before you reach the farm buildings take the path diversion to the left, and aim for the far right field corner and onto another farm track. Cross a minor road then climb up to the tree line and the National Trust land of Bickerton Hill.

The Fly Agaric (*Amanita muscaria*) is one of Britain's best known fungi (toadstool). It has a red cover with white flecks, and typically occurs with Birch trees. It is widespread in Cheshire. It is VERY POISONOUS.

There is little wilderness left in Britain and therefore good walking areas have, almost invariably, already attracted a defined walk or trail. This is true in this lovely walking area, with much of the route up to the south of

GR SJ 500 521

Larkton
Hall

175

Pool

Manor
House

174

Tarporley also figuring in the Sandstone Trail long distance walk.

To continue the GEW, once in the trees turn left on a track, and continue on this at the south end of Bickerton Hill until you reach an open area. The Sandstone Trail turns left, but you should turn right and climb up (through a gate) until you reach the top of this coll. Now there is a crossroads of paths. Turn right and follow the Sandstone Trail sign, and climb uphill again. Suddenly views open up to the northwest. You can see the oil refinery at Stanlow and, if visibility is good, you will see a black tower on the left of a low land mass – this is the Liverpool Anglican Cathedral about 43km away. Leave the trees and climb through Bilberry bushes (known to many people in the north as Wimberry) to the top of Larkton Hill. Wonderful views now open up, with a sea of green all the way to the Welsh hills, the Dee estuary, the Wirral peninsula – and Liverpool way off in the distance. The National Trust have erected a sign on the top of Larkton Hill —

LARKTON HILL
A property of the NT. Given by Mr Ian Scott
Hawke Dennis in 1982 in memory of his
mother, Mrs Mary Scott Dennis (nee Macfie).
The Area in front of you is Maiden Castle, a hill fort of
the Iron age which has 2 ramparts, each with an
external ditch, with a cliff forming the western edge of
the settlement. There is a single entrance, with
inturned defensive banks, into the interior. The ram-
parts were formed of stone and earth, held together
with timber lacing. Scientific dating suggests that hill-
fort was occupied around two thousand years ago.

From the top of Larkton Hill go on through the ramparts. There are now cliffs on the west side. Although you are on Larkton Hill the whole 'slab' of rock is usually called Bickerton Hill, although Bickerton Hill itself is at the north end of the 'slab'. This seems to be an area for signs, with a private lament now sited on the hill. Kitty and her husband obviously enjoyed both North Wales and Ardnamurchan —

TO KITTY
WHEN UP THE CERRIG LLYN I GAZE
I'LL THINK OF YOU AND OTHER DAYS
OF ROCKS AND STONES
AND FALLS DULL ROARIN'
OF HEATHERED FELLS
AND BLOOD RED ROWAN
THE STONES I'VE SEEN
WITH YOU, MY DEAR
THE DISTANT VIEWS
AND WATERS CLEAR
ALL THESE I'LL SEE AND
THINK THEM POORER
NOW THAT I LACK YOU, MY DEAR

GAZING FROM ARDNAMURCHAN
POINT TO THE HEBRIDES
THE WIND WITH GENTLENESS
DID TOUCH THE TREES
AND TO OUR EARS DID BRING THE
SOUGH AND SIGH
ON SHELVING PEBBLY SHORE OF
GENTLY MOVING SEA
AND SIGHT OF WEED TO AGELESS
ROCK HELD FAST
WHOSE DARK GREEN FRONDS DID
DRIFT AND SWAY
ON DYING WAVELETS GENTLY
FALLING
AND ROSE AND FELL ON WHISPERING
MURMURING SANDS
AND TO US CAME THOSE SCENTS OF
SEA AND HILL
STEALING O'ER THE BAYS FROM PUR-
PLE HEADLANDS
WITH FRAGRANCE RARE OF MYRTLE,

THYME AND HEATHER
AND TO US CAME A THANKFULNESS,
O LORD
THAT THESE AND MANY
OTHER PRECIOUS GIFTS
OF SIGHT AND SOUND
AND SCENT AND SENSE
BY THEE ARE THERE
AND GIFTED FOR OUR PLEASURE
ALDW

For those of you who are complete Sassenachs, the Ardnamurchan peninsula is in northwest Scotland. Ardnamurchan Point is the furthest west point of the British mainland, being some 43km further west than Land's End.

Follow the distinct trail along to the north end of the hill. You can see why the trail in this area is called the Sandstone Trail as you walk along on sand. Keep to the signs for 'Beeston' when the path turns left. Bickerton and Peckforton hills can now be seen as islands rising from the Cheshire plain, and little imagination is needed to see them as islands surrounded by a large sea. You finally exit at the north end of the hill, and the National Trust property, onto a minor road.

Turn left to pass the Holy Trinity Church of Bickerton, and reach a road junction. Go straight across onto Brunty Bank, and continue to its junction with the A534. Turn left for five metres, then right along a lane. Walk uphill until the tarmac track branches left, and carry on ahead on the signposted farm track. This used to be a copper mining area, but all activity closed down many years ago. At Chiflik Farm carry on the track to the right of Tower Wood, follow it as it bends left, then enter the fringe of the wood. Once you have reached the top of the escarpment the views to the west and southwest are excellent, especially of Bickerton Hill to the south. Very confusingly, although you are looking at Bickerton Hill, you are also standing on

Trig Point on Bickerton Hill

clear path north along the escarpment. Shortly after the trig point a footpath branches off down to the left – ignore this and climb a large 'step' to keep on top of the escarpment. This is a very fine ridge walk. Unexpectedly the path, and the wood, end at a kissing gate and you turn right onto a wide earth track with The Bungalow to the left. Walk along the access road to a T-junction with Coppermine Lane.

Go straight across the lane into a field. You are now walking in a southeast direction, and looking out onto the 'flat' Cheshire Plain. At the end of the field go through a gate into woods, and turn half-left to head for Bulkeley Hill (the whole range is called Peckforton Hill, with individual hill names). Bear right with the track and pass a covered reservoir. There is now an escarpment to the right.

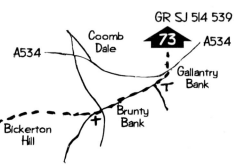

another Bickerton Hill! Some of the cliff scenery here is quite spectacular, especially at Musket's Hole. Following the path brings you to the triangulation point at Raw Head at 227 metres. Trig points are usually a straightforward piece of concrete, but this one is decorated with a shell motif. The woods here and, further north on Peckforton Hill, are thickly covered in parts with Oak trees.

Carry on the

When you reach a fork take the left one down to the wood's edge, then turn right on a wide track. After 200 metres you reach a T-junction at a farm. Turn left for 20 metres, then right over a stile. Follow the stone wall on the right, with the hill beyond. Keep the wall on the right and ignore other paths as they go off in different directions. The trees give way to fields, and the wall becomes a fence, but still carry on the same line until a tarmac road is reached (leading to Higher Burwardsley). Turn left onto the road for 100 metres and then right at a house.

Follow the road for 150 metres until it bends

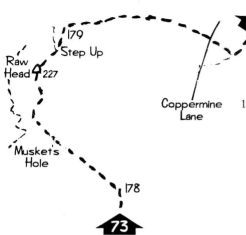

tinue on this path to a metalled minor road, with houses on the far side. Turn right for 300 metres until you reach Moat House Farm (now a number of house/barn conversions). The official route of the GEW is —

1. as you pass the farm turn left onto a track, and after 100 metres turn half-right just before you reach a large barn. Head to the right of a house that can be seen at the base of the dip between Castle Hill (with Beeston Castle on top) and Ettley Hill to its right. Go across a crop field and negotiate a fence at the other side, then a small stream, then another fence and strike out across a field for the house;

or

2. the above path may still be blocked (as it is in 1996). Therefore, from Moat House Farm, carry on the main track to meet the main road in 400 metres. In the corner of

left, and go straight ahead through a gate, to follow the right hedge/wall. From this point Liverpool Cathedral seems much clearer (on a clear day!). Go through a gate and onto a path through woods. Soon the path bends half-left to go downhill and joins a track near the base of the contours. Turn right and con-

Beeston Castle

the junction, to your left, take the footpath through two fields, over a stile and footbridge, and cross a field to arrive at the right side of the house mentioned above.

With either of the routes above, halfway to Castle Hill, if you look back, you will see Peckforton Castle. All the way along the Peckforton hills this is a sight which has been denied, but now you can see the castle in all its glory. The castle is 'modern', having been built as a house for the first Lord Tollemache between 1844 and 1850.

Once you have arrived at the house, cross the road to enter a wood. Go uphill and bear left to meet, and go right along, a stone wall. You soon arrive at the car park for visitors to Beeston Castle. Go along the road to the castle entrance (ice creams etc are available).

The village of Beeston, to the southeast, is dominated by the castle which is built on a sandstone outcrop commanding the Tarporley gap to the north. The hilltop was used by Neolithic tribes, and then became a fortified site in the Bronze Age. It was occupied by the Romans. In 1220 Ranulf de Blundeville ordered the building of the castle. The castle was used by King Henry III in 1241 to hold Welsh prisoners, and by 1303 was in need of rebuilding. The castle well is said to be 365 feet deep (111 metres) which says a lot for the engineering skills of the craftsmen in the olden days. There is a record of the garrison strength in 1312 being one Governor, two Squires and six Bowmen, but in times of conflict this would be rapidly increased. There is quite a story of deeds performed in the English Civil War, with an attack by Royalist commandos – you will have to visit the castle to hear more! The ruined castle was taken over in 1959 by the Ministry of Public Buildings and Works, which later became English Heritage, and who now welcome visitors daily in the season.

From the castle entrance go down the road to pass Castlegate Farm on the right, then after a further 200 metres turn right over a stile. Follow the fence on the right, and half way through the second field bear 30 degrees left to go under a railway bridge – an actual working line! (The main line from Chester to Crewe)   Follow the left fence to the

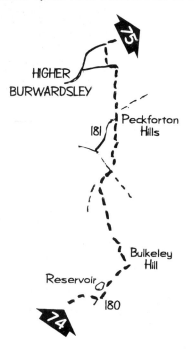

Wharton's Lock, Shropshire Union Canal

Shropshire Union Canal. This is a well used pleasure canal, and you can spend much time watching the boats negotiate Wharton's Lock. Cross the bridge at the lock, and a stile to follow the left hedge to Huxley Lane. Cross the lane and three fields to arrive on Pudding Lane. The Sandstone Trail leaves you here to carry on its way to Frodsham. Turn right for 70 metres, then left over a stile, and aim for the far left field corner. Cross the double stile and footbridge, then

turn 30 degrees left to cross the next field. Go over a stile into the next field and keep on the same line to the limit of the left hedge. At this point turn left and follow the left hedge to a stile. Cross three more fields and a footbridge onto Crib Lane.

Turn right to walk towards the hamlet of Birch Heath, but 100 metres past two cottages on your left, turn left over a stile. Follow the right hedge to a stile, then cross a small field to enter a larger field. Turn half-right to climb up the field centre, and go between a hedge on the left and an old quarry on the right. Just past the quarry is a stile in the left hedge. Tarporley is now looming large ahead of you. Continue, with the hedge now on your right, to reach the A49 Tarporley bypass. Cross with care, and then follow the left hedge, to go over a stile on the left 30 metres before the end of

Redhill Cottages

77

Crib Lane

185

HAND GREEN

Whartons Lock

FB

184

Castlegate Farm

Beeston Castle

Car Park

House

Ettley Hill

GEW

183

70

Alt Route

Moat House Farm

Peckforton Castle

GR SJ 534 583

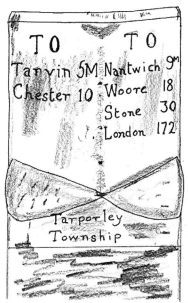

Milestone in Tarporley

Beeston Castle

the field. Follow the right hedge to go through the metal gate of the graveyard of St Helen's Church, and onto the main street of Tarporley.

GR SJ 554 625

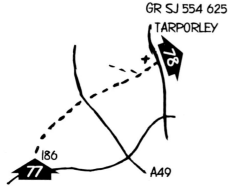

The church is dedicated to St Helen, mother of the Roman Emperor Constantine who was the first Christian Emperor of Rome. Her husband, Emperor Constantius, died at York in 306. The church was extensively restored in the 19th Century, but has 14th century nave

arcades and 15th century chancel chapels. There is also an 1891 wrought iron screen around some 16th century Italian church gates.

North of the church is Salterswell House. There is a well in the wall where salters from Nantwich would stop to water their laden pack horses.

The name Tarporley means "a pear wood near a hill called Torr". The town was settled in Roman times.

There is a story of a ghost which is sometimes seen on the road south, going toward Tiverton. An old man and his dog were hit and killed during a storm, by a coach and horses in the 19th century.

The Earl of Haddington founded the Tarporley fire brigade in 1869. It was the first voluntary fire brigade in the country.

THIRTEEN
Tarporley - Church Minshull
(10 miles or 16 km)

From the road outside St Helen's Church turn right for 50 metres, and then left on Park Road.   Pass the fire station, telephone exchange and school and, as the road turns sharp left, you should turn sharp right. Follow the left fence (with golf course to left) to reach the road at Cobblers Cross. This name has some significance as will be explained later. Turn left for 100 metres, then right on an access drive to a house. Beyond the house go over a stile onto a footpath for 25 metres, to meet the tarmac paths of what is now the Portal Golf and Country Club. Turn right on a path to pass the clubhouse entrance.

the cross commemorating the battle of Agincourt. The date on the cross is MCDIV (1404), but as we, perhaps, all know from our school days the battle of Agincourt was fought near Calais on the 24th October 1415 (St Crispin's day). In Roman numerals this would be MCDXV, so perhaps the general got it wrong when he gave his instructions to the stonemason.   The reverse of the cross is engraved "St Crispin" who is the patron saint

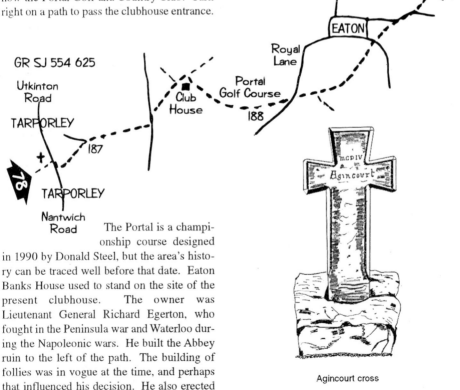

The Portal is a championship course designed in 1990 by Donald Steel, but the area's history can be traced well before that date. Eaton Banks House used to stand on the site of the present clubhouse.   The owner was Lieutenant General Richard Egerton, who fought in the Peninsula war and Waterloo during the Napoleonic wars. He built the Abbey ruin to the left of the path. The building of follies was in vogue at the time, and perhaps that influenced his decision. He also erected

Agincourt cross

Chapel Folly

of Cobblers – hence Cobblers Cross.

The Earl of Haddington built Arderne Hall in Victorian days to replace Eaton Banks. The hall was demolished in 1959.

As you see the chapel folly on the left, turn right around the present clubhouse on what is now a tarmaced golf buggy drive. Follow the drive as it wends through the course. The slight rise in land to the left is called Eaton Bank. 200 metres before the drive ends at a cottage on a road, turn right across the fairway for 100 metres to find a stile onto Royal Lane.

Cross the road and go over a stile opposite, then pass through one field with the hedge to the left. 200 metres into a second field go over a stile on the left, and head diagonally right across a field to a stile 50 metres to the right of the far corner. Turn left for 50 metres and go over a stile into another field. Aim across the field to a house whose upper storey only is visible from this point, and pass to its left onto a lane.

You can visit the village of Eaton by turning 100 metres left from this point. The name is Anglo Saxon and means "a settlement or village by water". To the northwest of Eaton is the small hill of Luddington. A wealthy Roman built his country villa to the west side of the village.

To continue the GEW turn right on the lane for 20 metres, and then left through a gate opposite the cottage. Follow the left hedge to a gate onto Hickhurst Lane. Turn right for 200 metres on the lane, then left over a stile. Go half-right across a field corner, and into a very large field. Strike out right across the centre of this field to the very far left corner, ignoring a stile part way across in the distant left hedge. Exit the field onto Dogmore Lane. You can now hear the tortured engines of racing cars at Oulton Park racing circuit if you arrive on a race or practice day.

Moss Hall Farm • RUSHTON • Oulton Park Race Track • Parkwall Farm • 189 • 190 • 79

Turn left on the road and follow it for 550 metres until you reach The Keepers Cottage and a minor road on the right. Turn along the minor road for 200 metres, then left over a stile and walk parallel to the road for one small field. Then go half-left across the next field centre until you are 100 metres from Woodgate Farm. Go over a

Turn right on the lane for 10 metres, then left over a stile. Follow the right fence, and over another stile onto Kings Lane at the hamlet of Rushton. Turn right and follow the lane for 500 metres to reach Parkwall Farm on the left. Just before the farm turn left over a stile, which takes you to the boundary wall of Oulton Park. Turn right along the wall and tree line. Should the racing cars be out, then you will certainly hear them, and see them, as they power around the circuit. When the wall ends bear left to find a stile, and turn immediately right to another stile – in effect, you have simply turned right and are now on the far side of the hedge. You are

Oak Tree Farm ■ ▲ Oulton Lowe Farm • 191 • Woodgate Farm • 80

stile and follow the left hedge, and then over another stile into a large field. Aim to the right of trees around a pond in the field centre – go to the far right corner, and over another stile. This really is a very featureless point of the *very* flat Cheshire Plain, and good maps are essential. Now aim 30 degrees right across a field to two stiles and a footbridge, and yet another centre field job. At last you can now see Cornhill Farm ahead, across many fields – head straight for it by crossing two more fields. Good eyesight helps enormously in trying to see the far fence stiles!

80 • Woodgate Farm

now heading south with a hedge to your right side. When the hedge turns right after 250 metres, don't follow it but carry on straight ahead across the field and over a stream, to a stile on the right of a small wood on the field's far side. Follow the right hedge from here to a minor road at Oulton Lowe Farm.

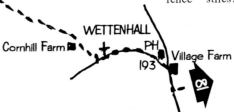

192 • Cornhill Farm ■ • WETTENHALL • PH • Village Farm • 193 • 08

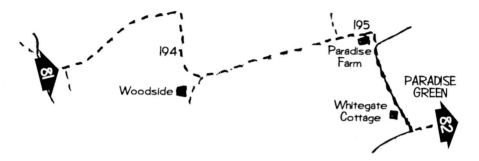

You feel you might be getting somewhere, but this is quite the most desolate flat and wearying stretch of the walk. Aim across the next field to a hedge 100 metres away, and go to its left. The houses of Wettenhall village are at last in sight. Reach the concrete and metal bridge over Wettenhall Brook. On the other side of the bridge go *up* the field centre to a stile between the house and farm buildings, and then a farm track to the road. You have finally arrived in Wettonhall village.

Turn left on the road and pass St David Church to a road junction and the Boot and Slipper inn. Turn right at the junction and take a footpath on the left after 150 metres. Cross this field at right angles to the road. In the second field still keep on the same line to stiles and a footbridge over an unnamed stream. In the third field still keep to the right of the hedge, and in the fourth field cross it 30 degrees to the right to a stile on the far side. *DON'T* cross the stile, but turn 90 degrees right to face Woodside Farm and head directly for it across the same field – it sounds daft, but that is where the public right of way is! As you near the farm head to its left side and follow stiles as they turn you away from the farm at a right angle. Then follow the left hedge towards the direction of Paradise Farm.

There is now a small radio telescope 500m over to the left. Go through two fields, then some 200 metres short of the end of the third field go through the fence on your left where

there should now be a stile. Turn right to continue on the left of the hedge towards Paradise Farm.

Pass the farm and turn right through two stiles to reach a road. Go straight ahead on the road for 650 metres to Paradise Green hamlet. In good visibility you can now see Congleton Edge to the east, about 30 km away.

At a road junction turn left towards Paradise Green Farm and over a stile into a field to the left of the farm. Follow the right hedge through one field. In the second field care is needed because there are two paths heading diagonally right across the field. One goes to Wades Green hamlet and one to Church Minshull village. Head 30 degrees right in this field to the second stile you can see, ie. the one furthest away. Continue across another field on the same line to go down to a footbridge over Eel Brook.

Almost at Church Minshull, the path now becomes difficult to find. Head half-right straight up the contours of the small hill and find a gate on the far side. There is a black and white house 200 metres away to the right. Go through the gate and to the left of a hedge to cross a field.

At this point the path splits – the GEW route goes half-right, down into a small dip, and then through to the B5074 road about 100 metres south of the church, but in 1996 this

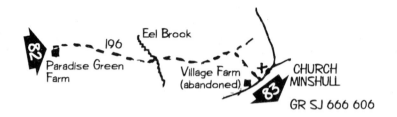

path is blocked. Until the route is cleared by the County Council you should turn right on a rough track to the abandoned Village Farm, then climb a gate onto the road.

Once on the road turn left to the church of St Bartholomew.

The church tower dates from 1702, and the rest of the church 1704. Many members of the Cholmondeley family are buried in the vault beneath the north aisle. There were earlier churches on the site. but these were demolished to build the present church, which was partially financed by a local rate levy and an appeal for Queen Anne's bounty. The village is not far from the Roman road from Nantwich to Middlewich, and may have evolved from that time. The village was mentioned in the *Domesday Book* as *Manshale*.

Wood Anemone *(Anemone nemorosa)*

FOURTEEN
Church Minshull - Brereton Green
(9.25 miles or 14.8 km)

From the church continue along the road until you reach a fork where the B5074 makes a sharp left turn to Winsford. At this point carry on eastward on Cross Lane. This road is too narrow for the traffic level, so take care. Go over the River Weaver bridge – the river is canalised for boats north of Winsford. On the left soon after this point is a house with interesting Dutch gables, built by Thomas Telford for himself, which he used as an office when the Shropshire Union Canal was being constructed. Carry on to shortly reach the bridge over the canal's Middlewich branch which was opened in 1833. The Shropshire Union has the Llangollen branch, which you have walked along, the Ellesmere (Prees branch) which you have almost passed

over, and now the Middlewich branch (originally used for the transport of salt and pottery) which joins the Trent and Mersey Canal at Middlewich to the main Shropshire Canal at Barbridge junction.

Cross to the left side of the road (for safety) before you reach a T-junction with Brookhouse Lane. Cross the lane and go over a stile. Follow the right hedge for two fields on the way to a small copse and footbridge. One more field is then crossed, with a hedge on the right, to a stile 20 metres left of field corner and onto the A530 road.

Turn left on the road for 200 metres, and then right along the drive of Moat House Farm.

Canal Dredging

Go through the farmyard and continue on a wide farm track. The track splits – the left side goes to Parkfield Farm. Continue on the the left where natural gas is stored in rock salt cavities. Over this stile, head in the same direction in a very slight depression (the

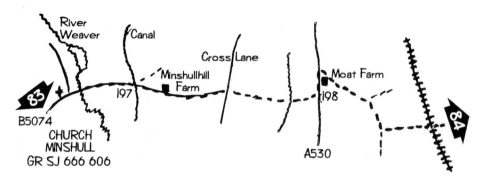

right fork to a gate with a footbridge going off to the right, *BUT* 10 metres before this on the left is a hidden stile into a field, which you should take. Cross the field near to the right hedge, aiming to arrive at the railway line some 30 metres left of the field corner. This is the main line from Liverpool to Crewe and all stations south. Cross the substantial pedestrian bridge. Congleton Edge is now much clearer to the east.

Having crossed the bridge follow the hedge on the left, and then go over a fence to turn left for 50 metres to a stile and a tree. Turn right here and follow a line of solitary trees (where there used to be a hedge) to stiles and a footbridge over the beginning of what becomes Hoggins Brook.

Carry on the same line (to the right of a broken hedge line), but slightly right to another stile. There is a fenced off rectangular area to

remains of an old hedge line?) and approximately 100 metres to the left of a pylon. Then pass over another stile and a footbridge into another field (just under the overhead electricity wires), and head across directly for the tower of the church at Warmingham. There is another stile, another field, and another stile to find a hedge to your right. Follow this line, with more stiles to reach a small stream – change sides to a hedge to your left, and follow it to the bank of the River Wheelock. Turn right along the bank and follow it to a gate onto the road at Warmingham. Turn left on the road.

Walking along the road you pass the church of St Leonard to the right. There has been a church here since Norman times. The original was replaced by a black and white Tudor building, and then by the present church in 1870, although the west tower dates from

1715 (and was regothicised in 1899). An 18th century sundial is in the churchyard. There is an old saying —

Proud Warmingham, poor people
New church, old steeple.

Church house dates from 1600, and Old Hough settlement (one kilometre northwest) is 13th century. Carry on over the River Wheelock and pass The Bears Paw inn on the left. You now reach Warmingham Mill on the left, converted to craft workshops, and its overgrown mill pond on the right. If you like old legends then there is one about the village. In Norman times a fierce Dragon roamed the area, killing and eating small children. It was finally slain by Baron Thomas Venables of Kinderton, first cousin of William the Conqueror. The event is commemorated in the Venables coat of arms carved on a screen in the Venables Chapel of nearby Middlewich Church.

Continue on the road past the mill for 150 metres, then turn right, and over two stiles into a field. Go through five fields. At the end of the last one take a short track left to a minor road. Turn right on the road for 50 metres, then go over stiles on left, and aim half-right across the field to the far right corner, and three stiles and a footbridge to turn you 90 degrees right. Go with the hedge on your left through two fields, and over a stile to the left. Follow the right hedge for 100 metres. Go over a stile on right, then straight across the field at right angles to the hedge and over a footbridge. Go straight across the next short field to a stile onto a minor road at Cherry Farm. You have now arrived at Moston.

Turn right for a 1km road walk. Pass over the Trent and Mersey Canal on the way, one of the great canals of England. On the other side of the canal continue walking on Moss Lane as it bends left. Albert Cottage is on the left, and a large industrial estate beyond the fence

Cheshire Stile near Warmingham

The Bear's Paw

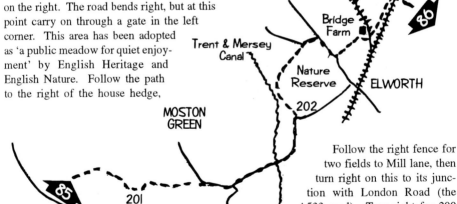

on the right. The road bends right, but at this point carry on through a gate in the left corner. This area has been adopted as 'a public meadow for quiet enjoyment' by English Heritage and English Nature. Follow the path to the right of the house hedge, and down to the side of the canal. The path goes along the canal, with a pool to the right, and perhaps some Moorhens and Coots in residence. Go round the north end of the pool to a stile on the right, and back onto the public footpath.

Follow the right fence for two fields to Mill lane, then turn right on this to its junction with London Road (the A533 road). Turn right for 200 metres, then left onto Elm Tree Lane. Pass a cricket pitch on the right, and carry on to the end of the houses. Turn right at Bridge farm onto a track to a pedestrian bridge over the railway track (Sandbach to Middlewich and Northwich). Immediately turn left along the left side of a second railway line (Crewe to Manchester) on a rough road. Keep the line on your right until you reach a bridge, which is crossed. Go across the field direct from the bridge. Bosley Cloud and Congleton Edge hill are now becoming very clear, although they appear from here to be one long hill. Bosley Cloud is to the left, and you can see where there is a slightly different colour – where Congleton Edge hill rises to this side of the Cloud. There is a small depression on the Edge (which the GEW crosses) and the Edge ends on the right with the folly of Mow Cop Castle.

To continue on this part of the GEW, however, on the far side of the field turn left, then over a stile into a large field. Go straight ahead using a line of Oak trees as a marker, but ***do not*** bend right as they do. Continue on a straight line to a footbridge over Small Brook, and straight ahead to a gate onto a minor road.

Cross the road and go straight across the first field centre and over a stile into a second field. Walk on the right side of a hedge, and at the field end go over a stile on the left. Turn right to follow the right hedge to a road. Turn left for 100 metres, then right on Pillar Box Lane for over 1km of road walking (but almost no traffic). When the lane bears left, turn right onto Bradley Lane with the Bradwall Wesleyan Chapel on the left. Cross over the very busy M6 motorway. The least said about the noise here the better!

204

Hilltop Cottage

200 metres beyond the motorway is a footpath going off to the right of the farm track. Go to the left of the fence/hedge for two fields, then 50 metres short of a tree line cross a stile to the other side of the fence, and then a footbridge over Sanderson's Brook. Take the path to the right and cut off the field corner, then over a footbridge and turn left along the side of a hedge. A very long field brings

Bear's Head

you to the end of the hedge opposite Duke's Oak Farm. Go over a stile and aim half-right across a field. Then go over another stile and half-left – to aim across the field directly for the black and white building of the Bears Head inn – and onto the A50 road. Cross the road and go onto the old road in front of the Bears Head inn at Brereton Green, an old black and white coaching inn which was originally a wattle and daub building that dates from 1615.

Brereton Green village has a general store/post office on School Lane (right from the archway, and first lane on left).

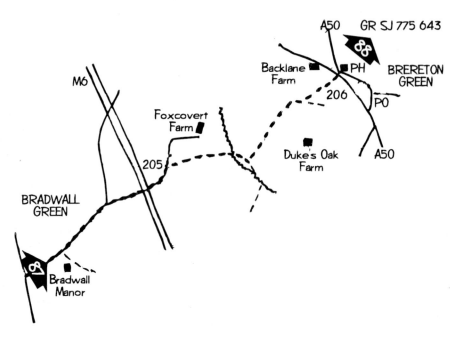

FIFTEEN
Brereton Green - Biddulph
(11 miles or 17.6 km)

Fifty metres to the right of the inn, pass under the archway which was the lodge for Brereton Hall, and walk along the tarmac drive. The drive goes over the river Croco – no sign of crocodiles! – on it's way to the church. Legend has it that a Brereton, in danger on one of the crusades, vowed (if he was spared) to build a church dedicated to St Oswald. He did survive, and on his return built the church about 1190 to fulfil his pledge. The church contains painted effigies (mid-17th century) of William and Frances Smethwick. Brereton hall was built by Sir William Brereton during the reign of Elizabeth I. It became a girls' school from 1937 to 1993, and then reverted to a private dwelling.

To the east of the church the main track swings left. Ignore this and continue ahead to North Lodge and on to a road junction. From here you get a closer view of the hills ahead – you will then be in hilly country all the way

into Northumbria! Bosley Cloud is on the left, and Biddulph valley separates it from Congleton Edge.

At the road junction pause for thought. Should you turn left, then in 300 metres you will come to the entrance to Brereton Heath country park (visitor centre and toilets). The park was once part of the Brereton family estate, which later became a silica sand quarry. It is now a large lake, with woodland and a bird reserve. However, to continue the walk, at the road junction the way is now over the stile, to the right of Brereton Heath Lane opposite. Cross the fields and continue to the lane near Smethwickhall Farm. The few houses of Smethwick Green here are all that remains of the ancient Norman hamlet of Smethwick.

Go along the lane ahead until you reach a group of houses, and find a grass track on the

Brereton Lodge

left between two houses. The hedge is at first on the left, then a stile is taken which changes it to the right side. Another field is crossed, then go through a gate to the other side of the hedge again. You are now on a farm track. Carry on to meet another track at right

then southeast around a sand quarry.

In pre-historic times Cheshire was a shallow sea (as we have previously stated) which is why the *"Wich"* towns of Nantwich, Middlewich and Northwich were founded to mine salt. It is also why there are a number of current, and abandoned, sand quarries in the county. The spire of Astbury Church can now be seen. The bridleway goes left before Bent Farm, then diagonally across the field corner and onto the tarmac farm drive. Follow the drive to the A34 road – referred to on main roadwork signs as the Manchester to Winchester road, which have always seemed to us to be odd destinations! At the road junction you can turn left for 100 metres to a post office/ tearoom, but the GEW turns right to Astbury village.

angles. Turn south (right) toward Lower Medhurst Green Farm, but just before the farm buildings look out for a gate on the left. Cross through the gate and carry on the same line to pass the farm and meet the track on the other side. A track soon goes off to the left. Follow this now straightforward route all the way to emerge on Sandy Lane. It would be nice to cross the lane and carry on in the same direction, but the route ahead is blocked at the main road and dangerous. The way, therefore, now turns right down the lane to its junction with the A534 Sandbach to Congleton road. Turn right for 400 metres. Cross over the busy road and onto the road opposite (signed 'Brownlow'). Approximately 50 metres on the left is a bridleway which winds its way east, north and

The village is famous for the village green daffodils in spring. The present church of St Mary is on the site of a much earlier Saxon church, and is one of the finest in Cheshire. The wooden ceiling, with pendants

and carvings, is 15th century The church chancel is about 1500, and it also has a 1290 leper window. The detached tower is 1366 and has a parapet spire. A tomb and several effigies in the churchyard are 14th century, and the ancient yew tree is over 1,000 years old. At the time of the English Civil War, Biddulph Old Hall (see later) was Royalist. Sir William Brereton (a Parliamentarian), stabled his horses in Astbury Church during the siege of the hall. The medieval stained glass windows and some church furniture, including the organ, were smashed.

Leaving the church, walk along Peel Lane to pass the Egerton Arms, the village hall, a very large vicarage and school. Then turn left along School Lane. The road surface changes from tarmac to aggregate. Take the right fork, and when the track splits again for Brickhouse Farm to the left, go right over a stile and into fields. Aim towards the right of the distant water tower initially, keeping the hedge on the left. Ignore the path going off to the left and, still keeping the hedge on the left, arrive at the hollow carrying The Howty, a brook running north to join the River Dane. Descend to the brook and then climb the 22 steps leading up to Astbury golf-course fairway. Across the manicured grass is a small wood. Watch out for the golf balls and aim for a marker just in the left side of the wood.

Once safely in the wood follow the broad track to emerge on a canal towpath. This is the Macclesfield Canal, one of the last canals to be built. Thomas Telford surveyed the route in 1825 and the canal was opened in 1831. The canal joins the Ashton and Peak Forest Canal at Marple, to the Trent and Mersey Canal at Kidsgrove. The bridge over the canal replaced an earlier swing bridge

Astbury Church

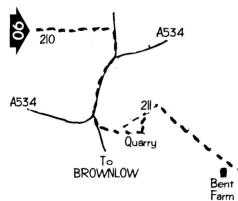

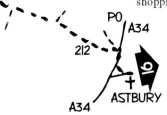

canal widens at this point to enable barges to be turned. After a short stretch on the unmade lane you reach a road (Wolstanholme Close), cross over to continue on Lamberts Lane. A further 100 metres brings you to a right bend to join the made up Lamberts Lane. Turn left and walk along to meet Astbury Lane Ends and Canal Road.

Should you wish to visit Congleton with its hotels, B&Bs, shops etc, the main shopping centre

many years ago, but new Ordnance Survey maps still refer to the swing bridge. ***Don't*** cross the bridge, but turn left along the towpath. Pretty gardens are on the far side of the canal, whilst on the left are golfers busy completing a round. The canal towpath hedge to your left has been trimmed in parts by house owners to improve their view!

The next bridge is a roving bridge. This was built to enable a horse drawing a barge to cross over to the towpath on the opposite bank, without having to be unhitched. Work it out – it's quite ingenious! Again ***don't*** cross this bridge, but climb the steps on the left to go up to the medieval Lamberts Lane. Then turn right to cross the canal. Look over to your left at this point to see the old canal warehouse at the canal side, and see how the

is 1.25km to the left down Canal Road. Along the way you will see the Moss Inn and Wharf Inn, and pass under the beautiful bridge carrying the canal over the road. Congleton town is on a bend of the River Dane – *congle* means "river bend" and *ton* is saxon for "town" – and was settled before medieval times. The charter dates from 1272. The town has a magnificent 1864 town hall and a number of pre-1640 houses on Moody

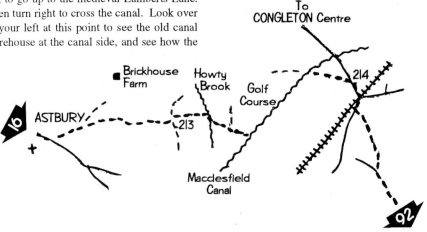

Street. There is some evidence to show that the town bible was sold in the 17th century to buy a new bear for the town —

Congleton rare, Congleton rare
sold the church bible to buy a new bear.

Turn right on Canal Road, and cross the railway line (Manchester, Congleton, Stoke and London Euston). Turn right down Moss Road and, on the left, between No 5 and No 7, go down the track for 100 metres, then climb the stile on your right, just after the track has veered left. The hill in front is Congleton

Having negotiated the first stile, walk with a fence on both sides to cross another stile. Then head half-right over more stiles and a small plank bridge to reach a farm track. Turn left and follow the track until it ends, then carry on the same line across fields and stiles heading towards the *nick.* Medieval times would have seen pack animals travelling from Congleton to the hamlets of the Biddulph valley via this route. Bosley Cloud looks impressive to the northeast, and Congleton town becomes a panoramic view behind. Keeping a hedge to the right you arrive at a path crossroads with a large signpost. Carry on the same direction over a stile and cross a small stream. Climb the field to go slightly to the left of the farm ahead, and climb onto Congleton Edge Road. Turn right and walk up the road. There are very good views over the Cheshire Plain with Jodrell Bank telescope, Peckforton and Bickerton hills. Continue up the road to pass Stone Cottage on the right, and eventually reach Congleton Edge methodist chapel with it's poignant First World War memorial in the graveyard. The chapel was built in 1855, and

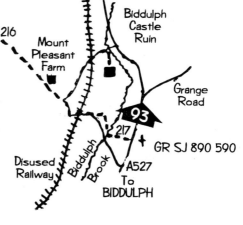

Edge, and you are aiming for the *nick* in the hill, appropriately called Nick i' th' Hill. Way over to your right, on the southernmost point of the edge is Mow Cop Castle. The castle is at 335 metres (1,100 feet) and is one of the earliest follies in the country. It was built in 1754 by Squire Wilbraham to improve his view from Rode Hall. The castle is now owned by the National Trust. Entry to the folly is free.

rebuilt in 1889.

Just past the chapel the road bends left, follow this over the summit (this is the boundary between Congleton in Cheshire and Biddulph in Staffordshire). When the metalled road shortly bears left again, carry straight on along the unmetalled farm track – this is part of the 90 mile Staffordshire Way, from Mow Cop to Kinver. There is a bridleway going off at right angles after some 100 metres. Take this downwards into a sunken lane which sometimes becomes muddy with the passage of horses. After 250 metres (passing through two horse stiles on the way) you will see stiles on both sides of the track. Turn through the stile on the left and into green fields again. Follow the left hedge. Across the valley can be seen the stone tower of Biddulph Old Hall. Down in the bottom of the valley on this side are the ruins of Biddulph Castle (which cannot be seen from the walk). The castle was

Penitential Cross, St Lawrence's, Biddulph

built about 1050 as a motte castle by the Biddulph family, and reconstructed in the 13th century. It was then occupied more as a residential hall than a fortress from the 13th to 16th centuries. Originally the castle had a ditch with an outer bank five metres below the mound top, with a second ditch and bank some ten metres below the top. The mound top also had a low rampart bank – each bank would have been topped by a wooden palisade. When the castle was built, the northern end of the valley would have been almost impenetrable forest and the castle would have had a commanding position at the head of the valley. Occupation ceased with the construction of Biddulph Old Hall in the mid 1550s, and only the outline of the castle ramparts and house now remain to be seen. The area of the castle, together with the accompanying Bailey's Wood to the north, was acquired by the Woodland Trust in 1994, and they allow public access to the site.

Returning to the subject of Biddulph Old Hall, the Biddulph family were strongly for the King, and during the English Civil War the hall was a stronghold of the Cavaliers. A raid was made on the parliamentary Horton Hall (in the next valley eastwards) and this partially prompted an attack by the Parliamentary Roundheads. Brereton Hall was indefensible and the Brereton family moved in with the Biddulphs to join forces. The hall was put under siege, and the Roundheads fired cannon from the east side of the *nick*, but this was ineffective. The cannon were moved to the south of the hall, and then to the east. Heavy damage was eventually inflicted and the garrison was forced to surrender its 300 men and 80 horses. The hall was never repaired, but part of the ruin is still lived in to this day.

To return to the GEW, follow the left hedge, and through stiles as they appear, to bring you down to the unmade road of Bailey's Bank. A visit can now be made to the Biddulph Castle site, if desired, by turning left along the lane for 500m, over the old railway line and into the gate on the right – just before you arrive at the A527 road – into the Woodland Trust wood and following the path up to the mound of the castle. To continue on the walk, however, turn right when you reach Bailey's Bank to walk to Marsh Green Road. At the junction is an old stone water container. This is thought to be a plague stone, where money was left in exchange for goods in the great plague of 1665. Turn left at the junction to reach the old railway line crossing. This line from Congleton to Stoke was opened in 1860 for freight, and in 1864 for passengers. The passenger service ceased in 1927, and freight in 1968. The track was lifted about 1972, and this stretch of the line now forms the Biddulph Valley Way (a route from Congleton to Knypersley at present, but ultimately open all the way to Stoke). Cross the line, either by the new road, or on the old road under the line, and carry on down the road. The road narrows and then takes a sharp right bend. At the point of the bend is a

Crusader's Coffin, St Lawrence's Biddulph

flight of steps directly ahead. Go up the steps and turn right parallel to the hedge, go through a stile and cross a field to another stile leading onto a tarmac path. Turn left and cross the footbridge across Biddulph Brook and climb the tarmac path to arrive at the A527 Congleton to Biddulph road. Cross over to St Lawrence church.

By an old tradition it is said that the Danes raided, burned and pillaged the church, which would make it a very old church site indeed. The first actual written evidence of a church on the site is 1190. The present tower is 1534, but the rest of the church was rebuilt in 1834. A penitential cross in the churchyard is thought to be 14th century. There are eight coffin lids with carvings, which may be from the time of one of the crusades.

You are in the north part of Biddulph, which has accommodation, a post office and inn. Biddulph town is 1.5km to the south, but there is a general store 600 metres in that direction.

SIXTEEN
Biddulph - Cheddleton
(11.5 miles or 18.4 km)

Facing the entrance to St Lawrence Church, turn left and walk along the pavement. The Biddulph valley, between Congleton Edge to the west and the rise of Biddulph Moor to the

Grange Road

Visitor Centre

Biddulph Grange Gardens (NT)

St Lawrence Church

93

BIDDULPH

GR SJ 890 590

Spring House

218

Spring Wood

Lake

Eliases Lane

Dew Lane

PH

BIDDULPH MOOR

PO 219

Wraggs Lane

Leek Lane

Trent Head Trent Head Farm

Springbank Farm

220

Crowborough Road

LASK EDGE

94

Greenhouse Farm

wife Maria, decided to move here from his parents' house, Knypersley Hall – to the south side of the town – in 1841. The incumbent vicar was James' uncle, William Holt, and he was moved to the beautiful house of Elmhurst not far to the east. James set about rebuilding the grange into a large stately home with 100 acres of garden. He was assisted in this from 1847 by his friend Edward Cooke. The gardens became famous and featured in the *Gardeners Chronicle* of the time. Whilst most of the area was a wild parkland, the 15 acres to the south of the house became a series of hidden secret gardens from around the world, with gardens from Italy, Egypt, the Americas, Scotland and, above all, China – the gardens also boast the largest gar-

east, was once heavily forested and occupied by a number of hamlets (you are in what was the hamlet of Poolfold now). The hamlets only came together under the name of Biddulph in the 1930s. The name Biddulph has been spelt many different ways throughout history, and some 29 versions are known. The area was mentioned in the *Domesday Book* in 1086 as *Bidolf*, the name probably meaning "Town of the Wolf".

You shortly arrive at Grange Road. Turn off to the right and go along this road following the right side pavement to reach the entrance to the National Trust property of Biddulph Grange Gardens. The large landowners in the 18th and 19th centuries in this area were the Bateman family. Biddulph Grange, as its name suggests, was a large house which had originally been an outstation of Hulton Abbey, and then ultimately the vicarage for St Lawrence's church. James, together with his

Lask Edge Methodist Church

den urn in the country, a copy of this (made from 6,200 wire coat hangers) was placed in the Hat Hill sculpture park at Chichester in 1996.

Fortunes changed and the Batemans moved out in 1871. The Heath family bought the estates, but could not afford the upkeep after the First World War. The house became a hospital and the gardens suffered, especially from the 1960s onwards from vandalism. When the hospital closed in 1991 the National Trust opened the gardens to the public after they had been restored.

The parkland was taken over by the Staffordshire Moorlands District Council and opened to the public as a country park. The house is still looking for a developer. The gardens are now known as possibly the finest Victorian gardens in the country. Do spare the time for a visit.

To continue the walk carry on along the pave-

ment, to pass the lodgekeeper's house (now the NT head gardeners house) and the house drive. The pavement now narrows considerably. As it ends turn right along a drive – note the old drinking fountain on the opposite side of the road first. The drive leads you past a house and then the almshouses built by James Bateman in 1858, and the old stable block on the right. You then reach a stile into the country park. Over the stile, follow the broad track as it leads to the visitor centre. The centre sells books, and has toilets.

Follow the main park track as it leaves the visitor centre to enter Spring Wood. You are now walking to the right of an unnamed tributary of the Biddulph Brook. Ignore the signpost for the Fishpool (unless you want to detour 200 metres to see the large lake). You now reach a bridge over the brook, and just before this on the right is the signposted permissive Himalayan Walk. Turn right to follow the route, which is on the right bank of the tributary, and pass over two wooden

Trent Head Well

bridges to reach picnic tables. The path soon forks, with the right fork passing over another footbridge. Take the left fork to go up steps through Rhododendron bushes and a stone stile onto Hurst Road.

Turn right on the road, and take the right fork after 100 metres as the road passes to the right of Spring House (with its tower). The road now turns sharp right over a bridge, but don't follow it – go straight ahead before the bridge (with a signpost for a path, and a 'No Through Road' sign). The track climbs sharply and swings left after 200 metres. At this point turn right through a stone stile (more a gap in the wall), and down into the wood to reach the Biddulph Brook tributary again. Cross with care and climb up the path opposite on the left bank of yet another tributary. The bank has collapsed in places and care must be taken, but it is a beautiful walk through this small strip of wood. The path reaches the head of the stream and crosses to climb an overgrown bank up to Eliases Lane.

Turn left, passing rocks on the right known as Job Wills Rocks, until you reach a T-junction with another small lane (Dew Lane). Turn right on Dew Lane for 100 metres to an abandoned farmhouse, and turn left here through a stile. Follow the right broken hedge. At the field end, marked by an old brick trough, turn right through a stile. Cross the middle of this field, aiming for the bungalows opposite, and enter onto Beckfields Close which shortly joins School Lane at a T-junction.

Turn left along the lane and pass Moor First School to carry onto a T-junction with Hot Lane. This is Biddulph Moor – it is not a village or parish, but forms part of Biddulph Town and Biddulph Parish. The Foxhound inn is 200 metres to the left, and the centre of this area is 200 metres right with a post office and stores.

Cross Hot Lane and go onto the tarmac path opposite, to bear right and reach Rudyard Road. Turn left on the road for 50 metres, then right into Broomfields (a lane). After 200 metres you reach another T-junction. Turn right for 50 metres to reach Hockadilla Farm on your left. The right of way through the farm and beyond was confirmed at a court hearing in 1994, but in 1996 it still awaits the County Council installation of stiles to make passage possible.

When you arrive (if a stile has been installed) the GEW turns into the farmyard to climb a stile over a wall (to the right of the farm-house), then follows to the left of a boundary fence at the rear of house gardens (over two more stiles on the way) and through a gate to arrive at Leek Lane, opposite Barrage Road. Should the route still await action from the County Council, carry on past the farm along Farmside Lane to turn left on Wraggs Lane at its end. At the end of this lane turn left for 200 metres to Barrage Road.

Turn down Barrage Road for approximately 75 metres until just past No 10. Turn right alongside the house on a signposted path. Pass the end of Highland Close cul-de-sac, and keep on the grass path to reach a foot-bridge on the left. Pass over the bridge and strike out directly across the field for 50 metres to reach a dip where the mighty River Trent rises. The spring seems almost dry, but does run all year – that is why this was declared the source many years ago. The old Biddulph Urban District Council, who erect-ed the edifice in 1935, was replaced in 1974 on administrative reorganisation by the Staffordshire Moorlands District Council, who placed the commemorative gate in posi-tion in 1996.

Retrace your steps to the footbridge, but don't cross. Turn right in the field and follow the left hedge to reach an abandoned farmhouse. Go through the farmyard to the left of the old house and on the short drive to Barrage Road. Turn right along the road and pass a path off to the right, and Bradda cottage to the left.

Carry on the road. There are excellent views over to Congleton Edge and Mow Cop Castle. When you reach a farm drive (and a path sign) to the left, turn along this to Springbank Farm. Pass directly through the farmyard on the concrete base until this ends, then go through the gate on your right. Pass through the field with the hedge to your right to reach a stile, and then follow the right fence again through the next field to a second stile. In the third field aim for the far left corner and a stile onto Crowborough Road. This area is the watershed of England, dividing water flowing either west or east.

Turn left for 100 metres and find the stile on the right just past a farm drive. Go over and follow the right fence for 50 metres, then go half-left to a stile to the left of a gate (ignore stile to right and the gate ahead). Once in this field aim for a stile in the opposite fence, 100 metres to the left of the far right corner. Over this stile carry on the same line, aiming for the distant farm buildings. This is the origi-nal moor of Biddulph Moor. Find a stile in a fence and still aim slightly left towards the farm buildings. The stile giving access to the last field before the farm is near a solitary Hawthorn tree. Once over this stile follow the right hedge to Greenhouse Farm, then go along the farm drive to Lask Edge Road. Lask Edge Methodist Church is to your right. This road on the top of Biddulph Moor gives views eastwards down into the Horton Valley. The valley does not have any major road, nor industry, and is unspoilt and beautiful. There is some farmhouse accommodation nearby.

Turn right for 30 metres, then left just past the telephone kiosk into a farm road. Keep on this 'road' to pass first Hallwood Farm, then Chatsworth Farm. The valley is some 3 km wide and three times as long, and is the home of visiting Fieldfares and Redwings in winter. The views open out as you descend. You arrive at The Ashes Farm. Then turn right directly opposite the farmhouse door to go

King's Chair in Red Lion inn

over a stile into a field. Cross the field centre, slightly right, to a stile in the opposite Holly hedge, and cross the next field to a stile in opposite wall. Horton village can now be seen 2km away down in the valley floor.

for the left side of the farmhouse. Go through the gate and cross the farmyard, to climb the steps and through the stile just to the left of a small barn (not through the gate). Cross a field half-right, aiming for the right side of the large barn of Grange Farm. Having reached the barn follow the left fence to a stile onto a road 20 metres right of a farm gate. This is the hamlet of Blackwood Hill.

Turn left on the road until it turns sharp left, and go down the second turn on the right towards Park Hayes Farm. The drive turns left to the farm to pass a house and arrive at barns. Turn right in front of a barn and cross a lawn into an open field – do not turn left to follow a track beyond the barn. Cross this field 30 metres left of the right fence, widening to 70 metres to a stile in the opposite fence. Cross the next field again about 30 metres from the right fence. As you reach trees on

The church of St Michaels at Horton was probably founded in the 13th century, and once was a chapel of Dieulacres Abbey, just north of Leek. George Heath, the moorland poet, lived in the parish and was buried there, aged 25, in 1869. There is also the grave of Mary Brookes, who died in 1787 aged 119. Horton Hall was damaged, in the English Civil War, by a Royalist raid from Biddulph Old hall in 1644. Another 1km beyond Horton, and in the same parish, lies Rudyard with its small group of houses and canal reservoir – commonly called Rudyard Lake. Kipling's parents courted and became engaged here, and when their son was born he was christened Rudyard.

Two fields now separate you from the farmhouse hamlet of Small Lane, but do not be tempted to head for the obvious farm gate down to the left in the opposite hedge (which is more of a thin line of trees). Head for the hedge some 100 metres to the right of the gate to find a stile and six steps leading through the tree line. Go over a small stream and head

the far side swing left to arrive at a stile giving access to a farm track. Turn right and cross either the ford or a footbridge, depending on water depth. Turn left up the track, ignoring the stile to the left. The track joins another going right to bring you to a small wall on the left which is only about four metres long. At the end of the wall go through a stile on the left (before a gate). You are now in a very long field. Aim towards the "imagined" far right corner. After some 200 metres a hedge line comes in on the right in the next field, and another 30 metres brings you to two stiles and a footbridge on the right giving access into the next field. Cross this field half-left over a slight hill. On the other side of the hill you can see Woodcock Hurst Farm ahead. Head for the right side of the farm to find a stile onto Gratton Lane.

Turn left for 125 metres to the second gate on the right. Go over this heavy gate onto the old drive of Mill Farm, with its name picked out in the cobbled drive. Pass the barns and go through a gate into a field. Keep the hedge on your left until a foot-bridge lets you cross over the stream to the left. Turn right to follow the right hedge. Keep on the same line when this turns, to another footbridge over the Horton Brook. This brook drains all the southern end of the Horton Valley, going southwards and eastwards towards the River Churnet and the River Trent. Just north of Rudyard, streams flow north and west to the River Dane and River Mersey. Over the bridge follow the left hedge, bearing left with it to another stile. Over this turn right along the hedge to reach a road. This is the road from Dunwood to Gratton and is little used. Turn left on the road until it turns sharp left. At this point turn right over a stile and follow the left hedge. Go over a stile and follow the hedge until Dunwood Farm is seen. Head for

the gate just to the right of the farmhouse. Turn left along farm drive to reach Dunwood Road.

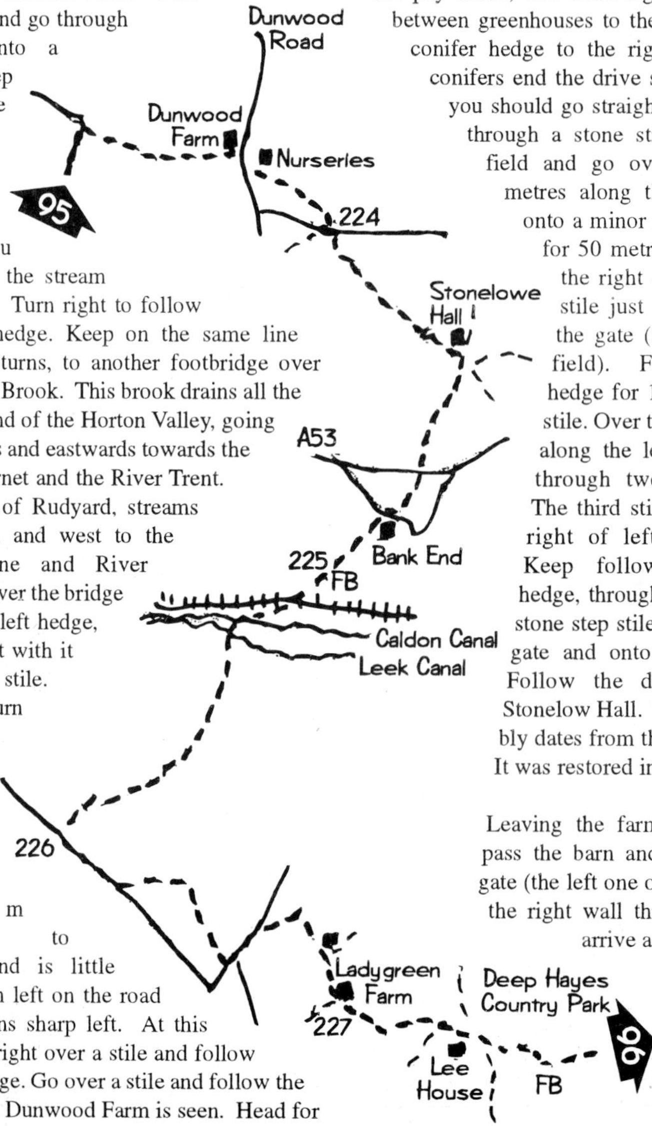

Turn left for 10 metres, then right through a metal gate and into Bancroft nurseries. Yes, this is a right of way! Follow the drive past the pay kiosk, and bend right to follow it between greenhouses to the left and a tall conifer hedge to the right. When the conifers end the drive swings left, but you should go straight ahead to pass through a stone stile. Cross the field and go over a stile 100 metres along the right hedge onto a minor road. Turn left for 50 metres to a gate on the right – go through a stile just to the right of the gate (into a different field). Follow the left hedge for 100 metres to a stile. Over the stile turn left along the left hedge. Go through two more stiles. The third stile is 50 metres right of left field corner. Keep following the left hedge, through a gate, then a stone step stile at the left of a gate and onto a farm drive. Follow the drive to reach Stonelow Hall. The hall probably dates from the 17th century. It was restored in 1866.

Leaving the farm, go south to pass the barn and go through a gate (the left one of two). Follow the right wall through fields to arrive at two gates giving access to the A53 road. There is an inn, and post office/store 1km left at

Map labels: Dunwood Road, Dunwood Farm, 95, Nurseries, 224, Stonelowe Hall, A53, 225, FB, Bank End, Caldon Canal, Leek Canal, 226, Ladygreen Farm, 227, Lee House, Deep Hayes Country Park, FB, 96

Longsdon. Cross the road with care to the right of the two gates opposite and onto a stony track. Follow the track to pass to the left of a farmhouse and onto an old lane. Turn right for 50 metres, passing the Bank End Motel on the way, and turn left on a path. Pass over a leaning footbridge, and then right over a plank bridge to aim for the bottom right of the field and a stile onto a farm track. Turn right along the track, and go over a stile on the right when the track swings left. Cross the field to a concrete bridge over the Endon Brook. Turn half-right in the next field for 100 metres to a gate giving access to the railway. This line was the Stoke to Leek line, opened for passengers and freight on 1st November 1867. Although the passenger service ceased in 1956, the line was still used to bring stone from Cauldon Lowe Quarry until about 1992. It has not been used since. Cross the line and through a gate on the far side. Aim half-right for the bridge to the left of the old lock-keepers cottage.

The canal is the Caldon Canal. One reason for building the canal was to enable quarry materials to be moved from Cauldon Lowe quarries to Stoke. It was partially surveyed by James Brindley in 1758, and on completing the survey in 1772 he caught a chill, from which he died. Brindley was not a good speller and he wrote Cauldon phonetically as Caldon. The name stuck to give us a misspelt canal name. The Caldon canal opened in 1777 and originally went all the way to Uttoxeter, but was filled in from Froghall in 1847 to provide a route for the railway. The Leek branch canal was built by John Rennie and opened in 1797.

Cross the Caldon Canal bridge and then the bridge over the Leek branch. The roving bridge at the junction of the two canals, dated 1842, is worth a detour. Should you wish you could take the towpath along the Leek branch to visit Leek, it is some 5.5 km away – but does have all comforts, and is a delightful market town. There is also a museum to

Leek and Caldon Canal Junction

1842 Bridge Over Caldon Canal

James Brindley, who was born in the area, which is set in a working water powered corn mill built by him in 1752.

To continue the walk aim for top right field corner and go through a gate. In the next field head to the right side of a barn (Hollinhurst Farm). Go over the stile and across the field centre to a stile halfway along the far hedge. Aim across the centre of the next field to a stile hidden in Holly trees. Cross the next field 50 metres to the right of a wall, over a stile, head for the left side of Little Hollinhurst Farm and over a stile onto the road. To your right (north) is the open Horton Valley, and Croker Hill beyond (with a BT microwave mast on top). Biddulph Moor and Bosley Cloud can also be seen. Turn left up the road, and then left along the drive of Hollinhurst Farm. After 20 metres on the drive turn right over a stile, cross two fields to the left of a wall, then turn right for two more fields to arrive at a road at Cats Edge. Perhaps you will be lucky enough to see a cat here! Turn left for 250 metres, then over a stile on the right. Keep the wall on your right initially, then carry on the same line to a stile

hidden behind a Dog Rose, and onto the farm track heading to Ladygreen.

Turn right and pass a house. Ignore a path on the left and carry on a track to arrive at Ladygreen Farm. Once you reach the abandoned farm turn left after a stone barn into an old green lane. Keep the wall on your left for 200 metres and, when the track swings left, leave it to cross the field and aim for buildings on the ridge. As you near the ridge the stile is midway in the large gap between the two houses. Cross the field and turn right on the farm access road to pass Lee House Farm, and take the left fork for 20 metres, then turn left into a field. Follow the left hedge to the field end, then turn right in a field to still follow the left tree line and over a stile to descend in trees. There are a number of paths here – you should take the second turn left for a short descent to a footbridge over stream. This is part of Deep Hayes Country Park.

Cross the bridge, and head straight uphill with a fence to the left. Over a stile go right for 30 metres, then left to initially follow the line of the electricity wires up an embankment.

China, Biddulph Grange NT Gardens

Mill Cottage, Cheddleton

Follow the clear path into a copse and over a stile into a field. Cross the field and enter a green lane going to the left of Shaffalong Farm. The lane ends at a stile. Cross a series of stiles through small fields to arrive at a line of Beech trees. At the end of the tree line head half-right to find a stile 100 metres away in a wall. Aim across the field centre to near the right side of a farm drive to the right of Hanfield farm. Cross the

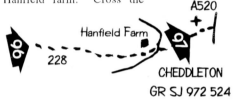

GR SJ 972 524

drive and follow the right hedge to a stile onto Shaffalong Lane at Cheddleton village. Walk along the lane into the village and pass the

school to reach Ostlers Lane and the old village pound —

1952 EIIR 1977
The Village Pound
This Pound was part of the village green during the middle ages. It was used for the impounding of stray animals.
The keeper is appointed by the parish council and the pound is now cared for by the children of the school.
C Staton
Pound Keeper

St Edward the Confessor Church was built sometime prior to 1214. It has stained glass windows designed by Burne Jones of the William Morris School. There are stocks on the church wall facing the Black Lion inn.

Peacock Butterfly *(Inachis io)*

SEVENTEEN
Cheddleton - Alstonefield
(16.5 miles or 26.4 km)

From Cheddleton village walk to the A520 road and turn left down to the bridge over the River Churnet and the Caldon Canal. Turn left to visit the Cheddleton Flint Mill. The mill and cottage are real gems. The mill dates back to 1253 and was originally for grinding Corn. Flint became required by the pottery industry from 1718. The north mill was built by James Brindley in 1756 specially to grind flint, and the south mill was converted perhaps in 1790. The two water wheels are of the low breast type, and powered by the River Churnet. A display at the mill gives the history of the site and the use of flint in pottery making. The oldest steel water boiler in the world is also on display.

From the mill follow the towpath under the A520 road and pass locks 13 and 14. The towpath is lined with Great Willowherb, Meadowsweet and Himalayan Balsam. At the first bridge climb the steps onto the road at Basford Bridge (with the Boat inn opposite), and turn left to cross the River Churnet bridge and onto the level crossing at Cheddleton Station (teas and light snacks).

The railway station was designed by Pugin – architect of the House of Commons – and was saved from demolition partly with the help of the late Sir John Betjeman. The line was the North Rode to Uttoxeter link, closed by British Rail for passengers from Leek to Uttoxeter in January 1965, but was used until recent years for sand transportation from Oakamoor quarries. The line has been saved by the Churnet Valley Railway Company, with trains now running north to Leekbrook.

Haystack Boiler at Cheddleton Flint Mill

Narrow footbridge, Coombs RSPB Reserve

Bridge over Derwent tributary, Baslow

Buttercross

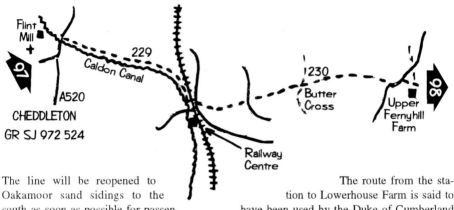

Flint
Mill

97

229
Caldon Canal

A520

CHEDDLETON
GR SJ 972 524

Railway
Centre

230
Butter
Cross

Upper
Fernyhill
Farm

98

The line will be reopened to Oakamoor sand sidings to the south as soon as possible for passengers. Trains are in steam on many days throughout the year. There is a camp site about 400 metres north on the road.

Cross the road to the dirt lane opposite the station. Walk for 30 metres, then go over the stile to your right. Climb the field, with the wall to the left, to pass Bridge Cliffe Farm.

The route from the station to Lowerhouse Farm is said to have been used by the Duke of Cumberland and his troops when trying to catch Bonnie Prince Charlie and his troops on their retreat from Derby. The two armies did not meet, but if they had we might have had the battle of Cheddleton instead of Culloden!

Cross the tarmac road. With the hedge to the right carry on to the ancient Butter Cross.

Flint Mill Waterwheel at Cheddleton

This was at the site of a market in medieval days, possibly moved here from elsewhere. The cross has an inscription: *"This ancient cross was restored in 1926 by William R Challinor"*.

Beyond the cross follow the right wall and onto the drive to Lowerhouse farm and a minor road. Turn left for 150 metres. There are Harebells here, and you may be lucky enough to see Linnets. Just past Upper Fernyhill Farm, and a farm drive, is a footpath going off to the right (marked to 'Ipstones'). Take the path uphill and over two stiles onto a farm track. Cross this, over a stile, and bear right to a stile to cross the corner of a small field. Go over the stile into a large field. Cross the field diagonally right, with a stone well marking the field centre. This is superb country, with Mill and Low woods down in the valley to your right. Pass over the far field wall stile, and turn 30 degrees right to cross the field. Swing left as you near a tree line to find the stile giving

access to the Coombes Valley Nature and RSPB Reserve.

Proceed downhill into the wood. If the sun is shining it will filter through the canopy of Rowan, Oak, Silver Birch, Holly and Sycamore. Follow the right fence to a narrow footbridge over Combes Brook. Follow the path opposite as it bears right uphill, and pass a small well on your way. The path divides Low Wood, to the south, from Spiritholes Wood to the north – it is an excellent woodland walk. The wood finally ends and you enter a small field. Cross and go through a gate. Turn left on a farm track and leave the track after 50 metres to go right along the fence into Whitehough Wood. This wood is very different from Low Wood, being comprised of Larch, Beech and, above all, Rhododendron. Follow the path as it meanders through the latter. Whilst the undergrowth is dense in parts, the path is reasonably clear to follow. Leave the wood over a stile and onto a farm track.

Lock 13

Cheddleton Station

Turn left for 70 metres, then right through a stile into a field. Cross the field 30 metres to

the
left   of
the   right
fence and pick up
a path through Gorse
bushes to reach a stone
wall. Pass through a gap and go
left of an old stone barn. Head half-
left to a stile (to the right of a gate) in a stone
wall. Follow the right wall, then leave it to go
through the stile in the opposite wall, then go
right of the Dovecote. Follow the left wall
past the Dovecote, and in front of
Whitehough Hall, then turn right for 20
metres to a stile giving access to the old hall
drive (now a green pasture). Cross the short
drive half-right to a stile giving access to a

field. Cross the field on the same line, go over a stile, then cross another short field to a stile onto a larger farm drive. Turn left.

Reach a farm drive (to Whithough) on the left, then count the fields on the right side. After the second hedge you reach a small stone wall on your right. Go through the gate on the right 30 metres beyond this point. Head

across the field to the left of a stand of trees on Summer Hill. This is definitely Staffordshire Moorlands, with the stone being sand or gritstone, whereas Derbyshire is mainly limestone as you will shortly find out. Pass through two stiles to get to the left of the

Curbar Edge

Dovecote Whitehough Hall

trees, then turn left along the wallside. The next 600 metres is difficult, but passable. Go through one field and a stile, then follow the wall and fence through the second field to White Chimneys house on the left. Climb over a wall, with a stile missing, and enter a third field via a squeezer stile with no gap. Follow the left wall in the fourth field. Turn left as the

wall itself turns left to find a stile onto the road. You are now on Ipstones Edge at 322 metres.

Turn right to the crossroads – note the misspelt sign for 'Cauldon Lowe'. Here you

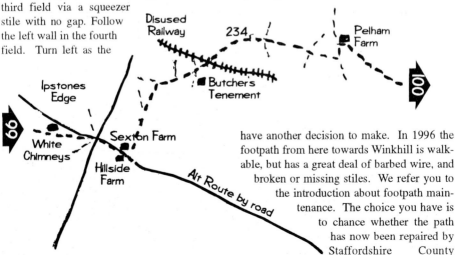

have another decision to make. In 1996 the footpath from here towards Winkhill is walkable, but has a great deal of barbed wire, and broken or missing stiles. We refer you to the introduction about footpath maintenance. The choice you have is to chance whether the path has now been repaired by Staffordshire County

Council, or do you bypass? —

1. carry on opposite the crossroad and pass Sexton Farm to the left and Hillside Farm to the right. After a further 100 metres go left through a stone stile (just before a house), and follow the right wall. Carry on as this is replaced by a hedge and a ditch. Pass through a hedge gap at the end of the first field, and a narrow stile at the right corner of the second. Keep following the right hedge through a third field (which changes to a fence part way) to the field end at the right corner. Negotiate the barbed wire to get onto a farm drive, and turn right. Pass one farm and ignore the right path. Keep on the drive until it swings right to Butcher's Tenement Farm. At this point there is a gate to the left and a gate directly ahead. Go through the one ahead, and turn half-left for 100 metres to a stile leading down the embankment to a rail line.

This is the Leek to Waterhouses line, one of the last full gauge rail lines to be built, and therefore one of the least likely to make a profit. The line opened from Leek to Ipstones in June 1905, and on to Waterhouses in July 1905. The line had only ever been marginal, and passenger service ceased in September 1935. Remarkably the line stayed open to Cauldon Lowe quarry until 1992 when that freight too also changed to road.

Climb the opposite embankment to a kissing gate and cross the field diagonally, to the right of a ditch and an old fence line, to reach a cross fence. Go over (or under the fence) and cross a farm track to continue in the field to the right of a ditch/fence. Next, cross a wooden fence and carry on the same line to reach two barbed wire fences two metres apart. Carry on the right side of the fence to a stile and barbed wire. Go over to change to left side of fence line you are follow-

Summer Hill

ing. Next, meet a blocked stone stile, and another blocked stile, before the path ends at a little used farm track.

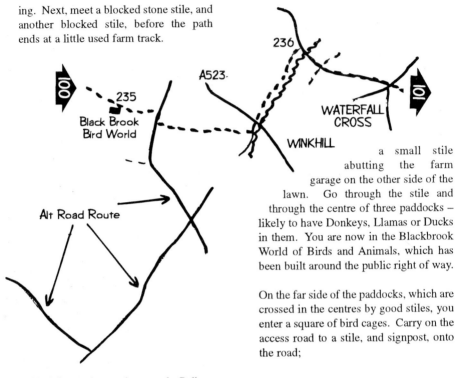

Turn left on the track towards Pelham Farm and turn right before the farm – in 1996 a huge Nettle patch – or carry on past the barn, turn right into the farmyard, and then right to get out again. Now head southeast (ie with your back to the farmhouse, turn half-left) to leave the farm and head to the right side of a stone wall to find a stile near the ditch type bed of the Black Brook. Turn left and follow the brook bed, keeping left of a very broken wall to reach the left side of a farm. Route finding now becomes more difficult! Go to the left of the farm, into the yard, and pass ahead between a brick barn to the left and wooden one to the right. Carry on ahead to see a more substantial farmhouse (Blackbrook). Find a stile and wooden gate giving access to the lawn immediately to the left of the farm itself. Cross the lawn on a straight line and find

a small stile abutting the farm garage on the other side of the lawn. Go through the stile and through the centre of three paddocks – likely to have Donkeys, Llamas or Ducks in them. You are now in the Blackbrook World of Birds and Animals, which has been built around the public right of way.

On the far side of the paddocks, which are crossed in the centres by good stiles, you enter a square of bird cages. Carry on the access road to a stile, and signpost, onto the road;

or

2. if you cannot face the above, then the present alternative has to be a longer route round the blockages. After passing Sexton and Hillside farms carry on the little used road for 2.4 km to a road junction. Turn left for 1,100m, then left again at another road junction for 900 metres. This brings you to the entrance of the Blackbrook Bird World.

From the Bird World turn right on the road for 100 metres, then left through a stone stile. Follow the left ditch for 200 metres to another stone wall stile 30 metres right of the ditch. Turn left along the wall for 100 metres to another stone stile, then half-right to climb the hill crest at 262 metres. Make for the standing stone, then go to the left of the walled trees. Now aim downhill to the brook and a stile onto the road.

Turn left for a short distance to the A523 road. Cross the road, and take the path opposite, along the left side of the river Hamps (there is a petrol station on the other river bank). Follow the river bank to a stile and footbridge onto the next minor road to the north. Turn right on the road for 600 metres to a junction at Waterfall Cross. You now enter the Peak District National Park – the first to be established in Britain. Turn left for 70 metres to find a gate on the right, just after two roads off to the right. Go through and aim across the field for a gap in the wall 20 metres to the right of the far left corner. Cauldon Lowe quarries loom large to the south. In the next field go to the corner of the wall 50 metres on the left. Do not turn left with the wall, but carry on the same line across the field to a wall stile opposite (the stone hereabouts is sand or gritstone). Next turn half-left and aim for the right side of a distant drainage ditch. 10 metres short of the ditch is a gate. Pass through and turn half-left to the far right corner of the field.

yard and church of St James and St Bartholomew. The church has 12th century bells and a Saxon cross.

Leave the church eastwards on the tarmac path to its wrought iron gates and the road. Turn right on the road for 100 metres, then left through a stile. Pass to the left of a farm silo and through a stile into open land. Cross straight ahead to a clump of trees in a dip to the left of Pike Low (a low 263 metres hill to the right). Enter a green track into the trees, with two stiles and an old clapper bridge. Beyond this turn slightly right and climb the contours for approximately 50 metres. Turn right to find a stile out of this beautiful wild flower meadow – a riot of colour with its Harebells, Field Scabious, Red Clover, Ragwort, Yarrow and Common Knapweed. Over the stile bear slightly left to the stile opposite, 50 metres from right corner. Keep on this contour through a series of small fields and stiles (or gaps). The first limestone wall is encountered on this part of the walk.

Arrive at a stone wall at the field end, and turn right along it for 50 metres to a stile onto the road. Turn right for 150 metres, then leave the road via a stile to follow a wall/fence on the left. Go over a stile onto the road at the side of The Red Lion inn at Waterfall.

There is accommodation at Waterfall. All facilities are available at Waterhouses only 1.2km along the road to the south.

Opposite The Red Lion is the continuation of the route. Go to the left of the house, through stone stiles, and cross the field to the grave-

Go through seven small fields in total and then turn half-right to a stile opposite. Then go downhill and through a gate to the old railway track.

You are now in a beautiful valley, known to all as Manifold valley. In truth this is the Hamps Valley since the River Hamps is on the other side of the track and flows north to join the River Manifold some 3km to the north. The river is there, but only flows overground after very wet weather, or in a few short stretches. This is limestone country, and that means hollows or passages below ground exist aplenty. The river, therefore, normally follows an underground course.

Waterhouses at 0920 – the connecting train to Leek left at 0930 to arrive at 1000. Despite all efforts the line was barely commercial, and closed in 1934. There are two cycle hirers at Waterhouses, and the tarmaced track bed is now a popular cycle track along the beautiful valley. The engine shed at Hulme End has recently been restored. Thor's Cave lies some 5 km to the north (a long detour), but it towers some 100 metres over the river and is probably named after Thor, the Norse god of thunder. The cave is about 10 metres high by 7 metres wide.

This valley once held one of the most scenic British railways. Previous mention has been made of the line from Leek to Waterhouses (a standard track of 4 feet 8.5 inches gauge). Behind the decision to build this line was the desire to serve the trade from Cauldon Lowe, but there was also pressure from the agricultural community of the valley. Whilst most of the country was now served by fast railway connexions, those who earned their living in the country were still stuck with horse and cart. The valley produce had to be restricted to butter and cheese, which would keep, rather than the more profitable milk. The opening of a line along the valley made a tremendous difference, even though the cost of standard gauge could not be justified. The line opened in 1904 as a narrow 2ft 6ins line, from Waterhouses to Hulme End. The line had two handsome steam engines. Special end on siding connexions were constructed at Waterhouses so that a standard wagon could be run straight onto the narrow gauge transporter truck. To boost passenger traffic, chara-banc trips were run from 1909 from Buxton to Hulme End to enable people from Buxton to entrain for a visit to Stoke, and vice versa. An early timetable showed a train leaving Hulme End at 0840, Ecton 0844, Butterton 0847, Wetton Mill 0854, Thor's Cave 0858, Grindon 0903, Beeston Tor 0906, Sparrowlee 0915, and arriving at

To return to the GEW, cross the line and the footbridge over the dry River Hamps, and climb the track to the right of Lee House (refreshments available). Blackthorn, Hawthorn and Hazel line the right side of the track. Another track joins, but carry on following the right side trees. Eventually the path bears right over a broken stone wall. Turn left to follow the wall and over two stiles to emerge onto a minor road. Go straight across the road and follow the right wall. You will probably see plenty of rabbits in the area, introduced by the Romans as a food source – they adapted and learnt to make burrows, and are now far too numerous. As the wall on the right begins to curve right, leave it and carry on the same line to cross the field, and join a farm track (coming from the left) at a gate and stile. Turn right on the track across the moor to reach Slade House. Turn left before the house barn, and onto another track to arrive at a wooden gate. Don't go through, but find a stile 10 metres to the right and walk to the left of an old stone barn to a second stile giving access into a long thin walled field. The somewhat conical hill to the right is Bunster Hill. When the left wall turns, keep following the right wall to reach a stone stile. Enter a green lane, and shortly an open field. Follow the right wall to pass an old limekiln on the left, and then a copse over to the right. Castern Hall can now be seen on the opposite valley side. Reach a stile in a wall, turn half-right and aim across the field for two gates in the far wall. Go through the right gate and walk to the right of a stone wall through one field. Then, after 150 metres in the second field, find a stile on left. Cross the field 50 metres to right of a wall, and over another stile go downhill on same line and onto a road to the left of Rushley farm.

Turn right to the junction with the farm road, then left and down to Rushley Bridge over the Manifold River. This river, like the Hamps, has an underground course in this area except in very wet periods. 10 metres over the bridge turn left through a stile and go half-right to cross the field and through a hedge gap to the top left corner of the next field. Through a stile keep on the same line to join the road. Turn left for 20 metres, then right up a flight of eight steps. Follow the right stone wall, through a stile, and then head direct for Castern Hall. Take the road round to the right and to the back of hall, and over a cattle grid. The road now bends to the right, but ignore this and carry on a straight line to a stile. Then follow the left wall. Pineappleweed is underfoot, giving off its distinctive pineapple smell as it is crushed. Bend right with the wall and cross into a second field, still following the left wall. Cross

a stile into a third field and turn 30 degrees right on a faint track, and bend left with it as it crosses the field (about 50 metres left of right wall), then through a stile to the left of a gate. In this field follow the right wall for 100 metres then turn half-left to get to the far left field corner. In the next field go forward for 50 metres, then turn left for 20 metres to a stile giving access to the ridge overlooking the beautiful Manifold Valley.

To the south of this point is Staffordshire Wildlife Trust's Castern Wood Nature Reserve. This is an SSSI site on carboniferous limestone. 240 plant, 40 bird and 80 butterfly/moth species have been recorded. The GEW turns *right* from the stile to follow the right wall, with a steep fall to the left, for a superb walk along the valley top. Keep on the clear path. Beeston Tor (and farm) are ahead to the left. You finally reach a stile in a cross wall, and then two stiles to the left to reach a minor road. Cross the road and follow the left wall. Go through a stile at the end of the first field and bear right aiming for the right side of Wetton village which is now clearly visible. There is a series of small fields with five stiles, through a camp site, to bring you to a road. Turn right for 20 metres, then left to Wetton centre. St Margarets' Church has enormous quoin stones suggesting an early building date. The body of the church was rebuilt in 1820.

To leave Wetton turn right onto the road opposite Ye Olde Royal Oak inn (signed 'Hulme End' and 'Hartington'). Turn right again after 50 metres and go down to a T-junction. Go over the stile opposite, and bear right across the field. Go through three more stiles then turn right to a stile onto a road. Turn left on the road. Alstonefield can now be seen ahead. Pass a junction on the left in 50 metres, carry on the road for a further 100 metres, then through left stile to cross field half-right. Find a wall and keep to its left, through a stile and carry

to the far left corner and over a stile onto a track to reach a village green (one of several in the village). Go along the road opposite to pass the post office/store, and then turn left to reach The George inn at the centre of Alstonefield.

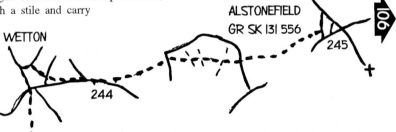

on same line, to right of a wall. After 50 metres the route swops to the left of the wall again. When you arrive at the next field, leave the wall and head half-right across and down the field to a minor road. Brook Lodge and Windledale Hollow are 50 metres left. Cross over the road into the next field, then through two stiles. After the third stile turn left. At the fifth stile is a step up into another field, and a sixth stile gives access to another minor road.

Cross over and go uphill on a clear path. After the second stile bear left to cross a field

St Peters Church is along the lane opposite the inn. The first written report of the church is 892 AD. The building incorporates elements from every period of medieval architecture, the oldest being fragments of Anglo-Saxon crosses. The aisle lancet is possibly 13th century.

The churchyard has possibly the oldest intact gravestone in the country, of Anne Green who died on the 3rd April 1518. There is also the gravestone of Margaret Barclay who died in 1731 aged 107. Inside the church is the Cotton family pew made for Charles Cotton senior. His son, also Charles, was a friend of Izaak Walton. When Izaak visited they would worship here. There is much to see in the church, and it is well worth a visit.

EIGHTEEN
Alstonefield - Monyash
(9.75 miles or 15.6 km)

Turn east outside The George inn to go along the Ashbourne Road and pass the converted Wesleyan chapel, for about 250 metres. Turn left onto a farm road, until you reach a fork – take the right fork into fields and follow it to a substantial stone barn. Go through the gate in front of the barn, and turn right through a stile to follow the right wall. Over another stile turn half-left to cross the field, and over a stile in the far wall. Keep on the same line to cross the next field, going diagonally right to a wall stile. Leave this at right angles to cross the field to a gate and enter the National Trust land of Gipsy Bank. Turn half-left to follow the path. Extra care is now needed as you cross the slope on the path, and then on slippery limestone. Follow the path as it descends the slope, with over 100 steps leading down to the valley floor and the River Dove. The river is the boundary between Staffordshire and Derbyshire – most people mistakenly assume the whole area is Derbyshire.

There are two sets of stepping stones to choose from to cross the river. In exceptionally wet times the stones may be almost covered, and even more care is then needed. Having crossed the river, opposite is the remains of a ram pump housing. This was originally built to pump water to the farmland above, worked by water action 'ramming' the

Stepping Stones over River Dove

water through. Turn left on the riverside path.

Much further downstream in Dovedale is a tourist haven with crowds of people at weekends. Here, further upstream, is peace and quiet with few people. After 200 metres Biggin Dale goes off to the right, but carry on alongside the river to pass from Mill Dale into Wolfscote Dale. Pass a series of small weirs. A footbridge on the left (not crossed) marks the change to Beresford Dale and a character change for the dale. The high cliffs on both sides of the dale are left behind and you enter a meadow. The path bears right across the meadow, then swings left over a footbridge (back into Staffordshire). There is a road ahead at this point, but the path turns right along the left riverbank. High cliffs return on the left for a short distance. The path soon goes over another footbridge to return to Derbyshire. The trees, which have kept you company since you joined the river, give way to an open field. At this point, almost hidden in the trees to the left, is Charles Cotton's fishing temple.

Whilst the dale has a number of names most people think of it all as being Dovedale. At the south end of the dale is Ilam. Ilam Hall is on the site of an earlier house which Izaak

Walton and Charles Cotton used to visit. Robert Port is buried in the churchyard, and his memorial has verses written by Cotton. Congreave wrote *The Old Batchelor* in 1693 in the grounds of Ilam Hall. Both Izaak and Charles praised the whole valley's beauty. Dr Johnson's 'Happy Valley' in *Rasselas* written in 1759, and George Eliot's 'Eagle Valley' in *Adam Bede*, written in 1859, are based on the valley.

The Beresford family owned land here for many centuries, and Charles Cotton (a descendent) was born in 1630 in the now demolished hall. He was a soldier, poet and horticulturist. It was at the hall that Izaak Walton, formerly a friend of his father, stayed with him. Together they fished the River Dove. They built the fishing temple in 1674 where their initials are entwined in a monogram over the door together with 'Piscatoribus Sacrum' (sacred to fishermen). The house is on private land. Izaak Walton's book *The Compleat Angler* is world famous, and was written in 1653. Cotton wrote the second part of the book on fly fishing, and went on to also write *Wonders of the Peak* in 1681 and translated Montaigne's *Essays* in 1685.

Follow the wide path across the field. As you pass the rise of Pennilow to the right, bear left down to

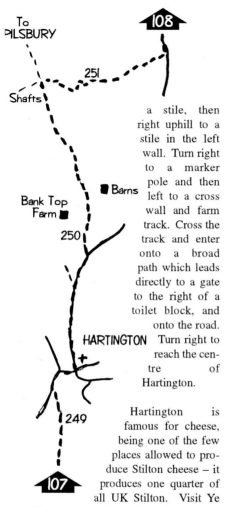

To
PILSBURY

108

251

Shafts

Barns

Bank Top
Farm

250

HARTINGTON

249

107

Devonshire placed a memorial behind the main door to Thomas Mellor "*He lived a remarkably sober steady life with the enjoyment of his mental faculties to the day of his death, the 6th December 1822, aged 103*". The bells date from 1636, 1677 and 1696, and the present clock is 1781 (replacing one from 1689).

From the church carry on climbing up the road. 500 metres brings you to an old track going off left, followed immediately by a footpath. Pass these by and carry on for a further 200 metres, until just past a house on the left. Then go over a stile on the left. Cross the field to opposite stile, and then follow a well marked path through fields. In the fourth field turn left on a farm track (leading from barns on the right). There is a very good view northwest up the valley. The infant Dove flows in the bottom, and is still the boundary between Staffordshire and Derbyshire. In the distance can be seen the two peaks of Chrome and Parkhouse hills. Follow the track for 70 metres until it turns left, then carry on ahead through a gate and bear right.

Keep parallel to the valley road and follow the right wall until it turns right, then carry on straight ahead (but slightly left). Keep on the same contour to follow a faint path, and go through a wall gap. Cross the next field to a stile giving access to a field containing old mining shafts. Cross the field to its centre, then turn right and head for two gates in the right corner. Pass through both gates and follow the right wall for 100 metres until it turns right. Leave the wall and go directly up the contours (following a faint farm track). Keep away from the right wall to find a gap 100 metres from its top right corner. Now bear right to a gate at the far right corner of field. Through this gate follow the right wall, until near the field end when it turns right and you go straight on through a fence gate ahead, and over a stile into next field. Follow the left wall as you descend into Long Dale. At the

a stile, then right uphill to a stile in the left wall. Turn right to a marker pole and then left to a cross wall and farm track. Cross the track and enter onto a broad path which leads directly to a gate to the right of a toilet block, and onto the road. Turn right to reach the centre of Hartington.

Hartington is famous for cheese, being one of the few places allowed to produce Stilton cheese – it produces one quarter of all UK Stilton. Visit Ye Olde Cheese Shoppe to purchase the produce from the cheese factory. There is no better cheese than White Stilton.

Leave Hartington by the Ashbourne road. Opposite the war memorial turn left up a road, and pass the church. Saint Giles' Church foundations are 13th century, but probably on an earlier Saxon base. The first recorded vicar was in 1298. The church is built of Staffordshire sandstone and Derbyshire limestone. The sixth Duke of

field end go through a gap to continue down with a wall now to your right, and over a stile **GR SK 150 665** onto a minor road.

Turn left on the road and pass Devils Bit Scabious in profusion and walk along to a road junction. Turn left on the road and pass The Croft (a house) and onto Vincent House (a farm). Just past the farmhouse turn right through the farmyard, then bear right and left onto a track going uphill. When the track turns right go straight on to a stile alongside a gate, and then follow the left wall. At the end of the first field go over a stile and turn half-left to follow the wall (through two stiles) to a road and Darley Farm. Cross the road and take the stile opposite into the farmyard. Pass the 1938 stable block and go

109

MONYASH

254

To **BUXTON** **253**

A515

Cycle Way

Moscar Farm

Darley Farm

252

Vincent House

108

To **ASHBOURNE**

through the middle gate. Follow the wall to your right, then over a stile and embankment onto an old railway. The route through the farmyard may be diverted – watch for signs!

This line was the Buxton to Ashbourne Railway, and went on to Uttoxeter. The running time was just under one hour from Buxton to Ashbourne. 500 metres to your right was the station of Parsley Hay, now used as a cycle hire centre. The track is another popular cycle way. The original railway through this area was from Whaley Bridge to Cromford, and was built to connect the Peak Forest Canal with the Cromford Canal. The Ashbourne route upgraded this track, but the Cromford and High Peak Railway (as it was known) branched off just to the south of Parsley Hay Station. This track also is now a well used cycle way, but used to be unique in Britain since it was used for freight only – and had several inclined planes worked by winding engines and hawsers, and also a 90 degree bend at Gotham Curve. Parts of this track were still used up to 1967, when they finally succumbed to the road haulage industry.

Cross the track, go over two stiles and follow the left wall. A gate and stile bring you onto the farm track of Moscar Farm. Cross the track and continue uphill, with a wall to left, and over stile onto the A515 road.

Cross the road and turn left on the far verge for 50 metres, then right over a stile into a field. Cross the field aiming for a point 100 metres left of the far left corner, to go through a stile and continue on same line across the next field corner. Find another stile, then cross the next field slightly right to a stile 50 metres to the right of the far left corner, then again on the same line across the field corner and a stile. In the next field aim half-right, then to a point 20 metres short of the left corner, and half-right onto the road.

Turn left on the road. Sweet Cicely (a strong

aniseed flavoured plant) can be found on the road verge. This plant is only found in the north of the country. You now have a walk of 600 metres along the road, to pass under one line of electricity wires and then reach a point about 100 metres short of a second line. At this point you will see, on the left, an old walled lane starting about 20 metres from the road. Go left through a gate and cross the 20 metres to the lane, where you will see a gate across the lane, and a gate just to its right. Go through the right gate and follow the left wall (with the lane on the other side) for 50 metres until it turns left, and then carry on the same line as before to go under the electric pole route. Cross the limestone pavement to an old stone stile in the opposite wall, and then turn left to a gate.

Through the gate turn right and meet an old walled green lane. Follow the lane as it bends left, and then turn right through an old gate to follow the lane. Next is an overgrown section and another old rusted gate (which may have

been cleared by the time you are here). Follow the lane as it heads for Monyash via a stile and farmyard onto a road. Turn left, to pass a small pond named Fere Mere, and reach the centre of Monyash.

Monyash was mentioned in the *Domesday Book* as *Maneis*. At that time it was one of eight 'Berewicks' of the Royal manor of *Badequella* (now known as Bakewell). The market cross dates from 1340 when the Royal Charter was granted. Water was, and still is, incredibly important in limestone areas because it all drains away into the porous rock. Monyash became very important as a centre of the Lead mining industry, now all gone.

St Leonard's Church was built before 1200 and greatly extended over the next 200 years. The tower is early 13th century, with external buttresses dating from 1225. Inside the church is a 14th century iron bound wooden chest.

Monyash Tea Room and Inn

NINETEEN
Monyash - Bakewell
(10 miles or 16 km)

Monyash to Bakewell is a series of contrasts, from open moorland to dale, and from solitude and quietness to people and noise. From Monyash centre take a walk along Rakes Road to pass Fere Mere again (and the path on the right on which you arrived). Pass Church Lane on the left. The road bends right, and at this point carry straight on, along the farm track (signposted 'Limestone Way'). The track forks after 70 metres – go straight ahead on the stony track.

The track is long and fairly straight, but it eventually bends left and right, changes to a footpath and reaches a stile. Follow the right wall for a further 70 metres, then over a stile and turn half-left to cross a field to a stile. You have just crossed Fern Dale, which develops to your left, and is owned and managed by the National Trust. Follow the left wall and go over the cross wall stile. Just before the next field end cross the stile on the left, turn right and keep following the same line with a wall now to the right side. Pineappleweed is again underfoot, releasing a marvellous smell of pineapple as it is disturbed. At the field end turn right through a gate, and left onto a farm track leading to One Ash Grange Farm.

The Grange was formerly a penal colony for misbehaving monks from Roche Abbey (near Maltby in South Yorkshire). Its old name was *Aneisc*.

Follow the track into the farmyard and turn left halfway through the yard to pass not one ancient pig sty, but half a dozen in a line, and then an old limekiln (with seats inside for inclement weather!). Branch right opposite the kiln to go between a corrugated barn to the left, and a stone barn to the right, to find a stile taking you down to a field. Imagine these walls being built by, or under the supervision of, monks many centuries ago. Follow the right wall as it goes downhill. The wall is replaced by limestone crags and you cross a stile to descend into Cales Dale. A cave is passed on the right side, and then you traverse below a huge buttress of limestone on the left. The path forks, with the route ahead going on into Lathkill Dale. Turn right at this point to go downhill to the bottom of the dale, and over a stile. What goes up must go down – or in this case vice versa, so you now have to climb 156 steps up the far dale side. Cales and Lathkill dales are a National Nature Reserve. At the top of the climb have a rest, and then cross through the kissing gate.

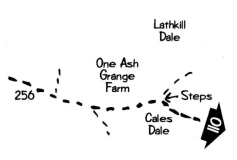

Pig's Residence! at One Ash Grove

There is an old custom in many parts of England that a kissing gate is where you kiss your partner – and there are many more to come!

Head directly across the field to a second kissing gate, and then up to the wall ahead, and a third kissing gate. Now go diagonally right to cross the next field to a fourth kissing gate, then turn left along a wall (to bypass Calling Low farm) to a fifth kissing gate and into a small wood. (look back to One Ash Grange, which looks distinctly monastic from this point).

Leave the trees via a gate, into a small field, then two more gates give access to a large field. Turn right to a kissing gate, and through this go half-left aiming for a point near the left end of the tree line opposite. Go over a stile into a wood and turn left. Leave the small wood over a stile and follow the broad path ahead. Pass over a fence and continue on the broad path to arrive at a wall, and stile. Over the stile turn left, and go over a second stile into a long field. Halfway across this field go right of a broken wall to reach a stile onto a road. Cross the road to go along the road opposite (signposted 'Picnic Site') for 150 metres. 10 metres past a car park turn right over a stile to enter a green lane. The lane passes

Font at All Saints Church, Youlgreave

with Bradford Dale down to your right). Continue on the road until you reach a road going off to the right (Holywell Lane). This is where you should turn right, but it would be a shame to miss Youlgreave centre – therefore, carry on the road to reach the centre, with a post office, YHA (the old Co-op building with the original department names on its dormitory doors), tea shop, general stores, and 'The Fountain'.

The fountain carries the inscription —

The Fountain or Conduit Head.
A reservoir of 1500 gallon capacity
erected in 1829 on the initiative of
Youlgreave Friendly Society of Women
to provide the village with its first piped
water supply from a spring at Mawstone.

Youlgreave was mentioned in the *Domesday Book*, and was once a centre of local lead mining. The medieval name was *Colograf* translated as "Yellow Grove". There is an annual well dressing ceremony in June (on the Saturday nearest St John the Baptist's day).

th car park and picnic tables and narrows to a footpath alongside trees, then over a stile into a field. Cross the field on the same line to go over a stile, and turn left to follow the line of an old wall with just the base stones remaining. When the wall ends continue the line on a well worn path to descend to a road. Turn left for 50 metres, then right into a sparse wood and field, over a stile and reach a second road. Cross this road, and turn left along the pavement. You soon rejoin the first road and carry on the pavement (passing the boundary sign for Youlgreave and allotments on the left,

Carry on past the fountain for a short distance to All Saints' parish church, which is one of the oldest and largest medieval churches in the Peak District. The earliest record of the church is 1150. This was to gift the church to the Abbey of St Mary in Leicester, so it obviously existed well before that time although the earliest part of the present building is Norman. There are some fine Derbyshire Alabaster carvings. The 13th century tomb of Sir John Rossington is in the Chancel, together with a tomb of Thomas Cokayne who died in 1488. The font is unique in being the only one in England to have a 'stoup' on the side for

River Lathkill

112

ALPORT

260

YOULGREAVE

YHA

259

River Bradford

holding holy water or oil, and was made in
the 12th century from local gritstone. There
is a peal of eight bells, the eighth carrying the
words —

I call the living, mourn the dead,
I tell when days and years are fled,
For grief and joy, for prayer and praise,
To heaven my tuneful voice I raise.

To continue the walk retrace your steps to go
down Holywell Lane, but then immediately
turn left onto Brookleton (a lane).   Red
Valerian grows in the crevices along the lane,
which soon becomes a tarmaced path and
bears left down to the River Bradford. This is
another river which sometimes flows underground in this limestone area. Follow the left
bank of the river to cross two small roads
(with an old clapper bridge to your right) and
keep on the river bank on a broad track
(crossing the river in the process). You swing
left and reach an old packhorse bridge – don't
cross, but keep to the right of the river and

Fountain at Youlgreave

Youlgreave Church Cokayne Tomb

leave the track. After a few metres you rejoin the track for 50 metres, only to leave it again by a stile to the left on a stony path. Pass a large limestone buttress on the right and marvel that the river was once mighty enough to carve out this channel and create Bradford Dale.

The track becomes tarmaced and swings left up to the main road. The river now on your right is the River Lathkill, and the village is Alport. Cross the road to carry on the path opposite. The path is now very clear and follows the river bank through several fields to arrive at an old road. Raper Lodge is to the left. Turn right to cross the river by means of the old packhorse bridge leading to Haddon Hall. Trout can usually be seen in the clear river below. Follow the path from the bridge as it bends and twists to reach the top of the valley. At the top go through the gate and turn right to follow the fence line to a stile. Pass the barns on the right and follow the right wall. Manners Wood is ahead on the other side of the valley. Keep company with the wall through three fields, and at the end of the third go through the gate and on to a farm track with the wall now to your left. Pass Haddon Hall car park to arrive at the busy A6 road. Cross the road and turn left along the pavement. In a few metres you reach the entrance to Haddon Hall. The original name of the area was *Hadun*.

The 1995 film *Jane Eyre* was partially filmed at the hall, which is said to be England's most complete and authentic medieval home. The hall is the ancestral home of the Duke of Rutland (whose family name is Manners) and was built about the time of the *Domesday Book* (1086) by Sir William Peverel, the illegitimate son of William the Conqueror. The family name changed from Peveral to Avenel, to Vernon (the Vernon family name lasted from 1170 to 1567) before passing into the Manners family name by marriage. The hall is mainly untouched by time, with 16th century furnishings. The walled garden is 400

River Bradford, Packhorse Bridge

years old. A Roman altar dating from 150AD can be seen in the hall, which was found near

GR SK 218 685
BAKEWELL
To MONYASH
A6
264
River Wye
A6
263
262
261
Raper Lodge

Bakewell. The Latin inscription translates: *"To the God Mars Braciaca, Quintus Sittius Caecilianus, Praefect of the first cohort of Aquitani, performs his vow."* The hall is open to the public from April to September on most days.

From the entrance of the hall, continue walking along the pavement for 250 metres to find a stile in the right wall (having walked mainly easterly from Tarporley, you are now at last walking northerly again). The stile is partly hidden in the hedge and has an equally hidden signpost. The stile leads you into an enclosed fenced path, passing through the Haddon Hall estate, and down to a large stone bridge over the River Wye. The river is very clear with large fronds of weed riding the current. The path goes on with a boundary railing to the right, following the meandering river on the left. The foliage is dense, but the path very clear. The beautiful Silverweed is pro-

lific underfoot. You reach a farm road and turn right along it for 30 metres, before going off left again through a gate. The way now follows a few metres to the right of a fence and, at a junction of paths, goes down to the river side. After a while you reach a footbridge over a river tributary, and the path now leaves the river to follow a hedge on your right. Bakewell church spire can now be seen. Follow the right hedge to arrive at a field used for the annual Bakewell Show (the first Wednesday and Thursday in August). The path now becomes a tarmaced drive (for show traffic) and leads to a bridge on the left, over a river tributary. Follow the 'Town Centre' signpost which leads you to a bridge over the River Wye. Turn right on the 'Promenade' alongside the river, with its multitude of ducks, to pass the toilet block and reach the main river bridge (13th century). Go up to the road (Bridge Street) and turn left to reach the town centre.

The name Bakewell comes from the warm Iron bearing

Haddon Hall

A6 To MATLOCK

springs found around the town. The earliest recorded form of the name is *Badecanwelle* meaning "Badeca's springs" – the name may have been a personal name, or refer to baths as in the German 'Bad'. There have been many subsequent spellings.

The Romans visited the area, as evidenced by the altar in Haddon Hall, but the area really came into being with Saxon settlers who tamed the Wye Valley wilderness. In 920AD

Edward the Elder, ruler of Wessex, built a fortress on Castle Hill. The owners of Haddon Hall were a major influence on the town's development. In more recent times, Arkwright established a cotton mill in 1777. This was the forerunner to improved water and then gas supplies. Jane Austen visited the town in 1811 – the year she wrote *Sense and Sensibility*.

Everyone has heard of the Bakewell tart, but the thing for which Bakewell is famous is the Bakewell Pudding. This originated in Bakewell due to a misunderstanding between the mistress of the Rutland Arms inn, Mrs Greaves, and her cook. On a day when important visitors were expected at the inn for dinner, Mrs Greaves instructed her cook how she wished the pastry to be made for a Strawberry tart – the egg mixture was to be mixed in to the pastry, and the Strawberry jam spread on top. The cook either forgot or misunderstood the instructions, and poured the egg mixture over the jam instead of mixing it into the pastry. What should have been a tart turned out to be a pudding, and went into the oven and then onto the table. The visitors complimented the hostess on the "delicious pudding". Mrs Greaves responded by telling her cook to continue making them that way. No less than five shops in the town claim to hold the original recipe. The pudding is very delicious, and a must to sample before leaving the town.

The parish church of All Saints has fragments of a pre-Norman church, but much of the present church is Norman, with the majority being 14th century. There are interesting gravestones and epitaphs. There are a large number of Anglo-Saxon stones which shows that there must have been a substantial church here before the new church was built in the early 12th century. There is much to see inside the church, with a 14th century octagonal font and an early 19th century table of church fees. There are also some brasses and delightful carved misericords from the 14th century. The church has a beautiful effigy of Sir George Manners, who died in 1623, and a monument to Sir Thomas Wendesley who was killed in the 1403 Battle of Shrewsbury. There is also a monument to Sir John Manners and Dorothy Vernon who were said to have eloped from Haddon Hall. The oldest monument is to Sir John Foljambe and his wife, and dates from 1377.

TWENTY
Bakewell - Hathersage
(13.25 miles or 21.2 km)

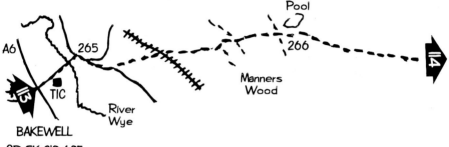

BAKEWELL

GR SK 218 685

Bakewell is a place which can exert its attractions for a long time but, having decided to leave, cross the medieval bridge once more and turn right onto Station Road, and immediately right again onto Coombs Road. Walk past the bungalows on the left until (opposite the showground entrance) you reach a farm road on the left. Go through the gate and up the tarmac drive towards Outrake Farm, but then through further gates and when the road swings left, carry on to follow the wall on the right side which soon changes to a hedge and takes you to the bridge over the old railway line.

The line is now the Monsal Trail, a long footpath route, but used to carry the main line rail track from Manchester Central Station to London St Pancras. The times varied, but most trains took about 5.5 hours for the journey and seemed to stop at every station en route, although some trains not stopping

The Medieval Bridge at Bakewell

everywhere took under four hours. A typical timetable was for a train to leave Manchester Central at 0724, stopping at Cheadle Heath, Chinley, Chapel-en-le-Frith, Peak Forest, Miller's Dale, Monsal Dale, Great Longstone, Hassop, Bakewell, Rowsley, Darley Dale, Matlock, Matlock Bath, Ambergate, Belper, Duffield, Derby and then down the main line to arrive at London St Pancras at 1302. The train would be a boon nowadays to hikers, but the line was closed. Manchester trains now go down the west side of England via Stockport, Macclesfield, Stoke and Stafford. The Central Station at Manchester is now the GMEX Centre for exhibitions and events. There have been suggestions that the route could reopen from Buxton to Matlock as a private steam line, but there are major problems in crossing the A6 road at Rowsley.

Having crossed the bridge, bear right on an old cart track and over a stile to cross the golf course fairway. Continue on the track to enter Manners Wood, named after the Manners family. The clear path climbs up through the wood, with Hedge Woundwort and Blackberries alongside. Reach a *fork* on the path – the right one is well trodden and is a concessionary path in the Haddon Hall estate. Ignore it and take the less used path, carrying on uphill to meet a transverse track (with a storage

bunker at the junction). Turn right for 20 metres, then left uphill to pass a small stone shed and arrive at a stone wall stile giving access to fields.

Turn half-right and head across the field. Pass a clump of eight (live) Oak trees to reach a stile in the wire fence. There is a stock pond on your left. Carry on the same line crossing the high pastureland (266 metres) of Calton Pastures. After 100 metres cross the left fence and look for the small ridge ahead – aim for a point midway between the fence to the right and wood to the left. You reach a stile in a cross fence, and carry on the same line for 400 metres.

Then follow the track as it swings left. The cottage ahead is variously referred to as the Swiss or Russian Cottage, but 200 metres short of it the path comes to a path junction and you turn left to a stile in the stone wall. You now enter New Piece Wood and walk along a farm road. At the other side of the wood you exit via a stile, and bear slightly right to a marker post in the field. From the post head for the left of a small copse. You are now in Chatsworth Park. The spire of Edensor Church comes into view ahead among the trees. Mark this well because the 'path' heads off down to the 'big house', and you need to leave the obvious path and head for the left of a wood. You may be lucky to see deer since this is a deer park. Going to the left of a wood, and the spire, will bring you to a footpath sign at an iron gate and 40 steps down to the 'main' road of

House at Edensor

Edensor village.

The sixth Duke of Devonshire objected to the village being visible from his windows, so the entire village was moved to its present position in the 1830s. The buildings were designed by Sir Joseph Paxton, who put together a catalogue of building styles with different periods and derivations. The church of St Peter (1867) was designed by Sir Gilbert Scott. The Dukes of Devonshire are buried here, and you will also see the grave of John F Kennedy's sister. There is a store and tea room. Walk to the entrance gate of the village and onto the B6012 road. Cross the road and go over the important small hillock ahead (following the path) which hides the village from the hall. Continue down to the beautiful bridge over the River Derwent – Derbyshire's longest river. Over the bridge turn left on the public footpath.

Note — The path is closed on three days a year. The Country Fair is held on the first Saturday and Sunday in September (or, if Sunday is the first, then the fair is on 31st August and 1st September). The path is also closed for the annual RAC rally on the third Sunday in November. If you really must walk this section on these days, then you should turn left from Edensor on the B6012 road, and walk along this to Baslow.

Over to your right is Chatsworth House, the 'Palace of the Peak'. The house has possibly the finest setting of any great house of England. Before the house is the river Derwent, and behind it the ground rises to plantations and moorland. Its history starts in 1518 when Elizabeth of Hardwick was born (known as Bess of Hardwick). She married her first husband when she was 14, and he died the following year leaving her a very rich widow. Her second husband was Sir William Cavendish, and she persuaded him to buy the estate at Chatsworth. Here she built the first house on the site in 1555. Bess and William's son was the first Earl of Devonshire – the fourth Earl was made the first Duke in 1694 for helping William of Orange to inherit the throne – and he started to build the present house. The house has a world famous reputation for its rich furnishings and decorations, together with elaborate furniture and large library.

The estate is not only famous for its house, but also for its gardens and parkland. The water on the moors has been harnessed to provide a world famous cascade, and the

Queen Mary's Bower, Chatsworth Park

tallest fountain in Britain at over 88 metres. In 1826 Joseph Paxton became the estate gardener, and went on to design the Crystal Palace for the Great Exhibition of 1851, whilst still working at Chatsworth. He was knighted for his work. Paxton had links with James Bateman at Biddulph Grange, and gave advice. The estate also has mature Chestnut avenues.

From the bridge the path goes left of Queen Mary's Bower. Mary Queen of Scots lost her crown and country after the battle of Langside in 1568, and fled to England for the protection of Queen Elizabeth. Officially a guest, she was in fact kept prisoner. Her first prison was Carlisle Castle, but from there she was moved to Bolton Castle. The Earl of Shrewsbury and his wife, Bess of Hardwick (the Earl was her fourth husband), were then put in charge of her imprisonment. The Queen was moved around several houses, but was kept at Chatsworth five times between 1570 and 1581 (in the first house). The Bower dates from that time and was probably built specially for her. Originally the Bower was moated.

Passing by the Bower, continue on the path which initially follows the river and then pass the White lodge and nursery. The path has become a 'road' which leads to an iron gate. Through the gate you reach a house on the right after 100 metres and turn right past the house, ignoring the path going off left, to reach a farm road leading to an old bridge over a tributary of the River Derwent. Turn left over the bridge to reach the green at Baslow. The road forks, but take the left fork to pass the car park and toilets and reach the A623 road.

Baslow is partially built around the Goose Green. St Anne's 13th century church has a very unusual tower clock. Dr E M Wrench had the idea to celebrate Queen Victoria's diamond jubilee by having one of the clock faces replaced. Instead of the normal 1 to 12 digits, the numbers were replaced by "VICTORIA 1897".

Cross the road and go along the road opposite (Eaton Hill), on the right side pavement, until it reaches a T-junction. Turn right on Bar Road. Lanes go off left and right, but keep on uphill. The tarmac surface is replaced by stones. Carry on along this farm road and bear right to pass a drinking trough (and path going off left), to reach a T-junction. Turn left to continue the stiff climb and finally see the Edges ahead – ignore the path going off right to keep on the stony track, now in open country. The 'road' becomes a path and you pass through a gate to enter the Eastern Moors estate. Pass an old quarry on the left and reach a fork in the track. Take the right fork to visit the Wellington monument. It appears that Wellington (known as the Iron Duke) visited the Duke of Rutland at some time and possibly visited the moor.

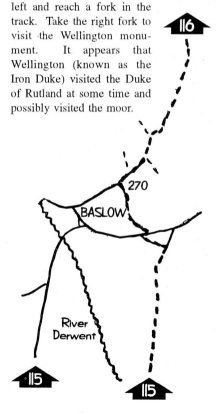

The monument was erected in 1866 to commemorate that visit, the inscription reading:-

Born WELLINGTON Died
1769   1852

Erected 1866 by E M Wrench
late 34th Regt

Retrace your steps 100 metres to the aforementioned fork, and turn right to reach the Eagle Stone, whose name is said to be derived from the god Aigle who could move boulders no man could lift.

This is a very old ridgeway walk, established by ancient Britons when the valleys were choked by trees and marsh. At this point Baslow Edge is over to your left and unseen, but to the right is Big Moor. The Edge stretches ahead, and you continue on the wide track to reach an old Roman road. Cross the road to continue on the track, now on Curbar Edge. The villages of Curbar and Calver are down in the valley, and you now see the sheer drops from the Edges – a favourite climbing area for many people. The Edge changes name again to Froggatt Edge as you see the village of Froggatt below. The village origi-

nally had 17 fresh water springs. This is a long and exhilarating stretch of the GEW. Surprisingly the Edge decreases, and you pass through a gate to enter a wood, but follow the clear track to drop down to the B6054 road.

Turn right on the road for 70 metres, then left through a wooden gate to enter the National Trust property of Hay Wood. Ford a stream and go along a section of old cobbled path to pass to the left of a car park. The path forks alongside the car park. Take the left fork downhill to enter Hay Wood and pass through a gate on a clear path. The wood is mainly Sycamore, Beech, Birch and Oak. Approximately 200 metres from the car park the path forks again. A well trodden path goes left downhill – *ignore this* and go straight on the less used path ahead, which climbs gently before becoming level (still in the woodland). Exit the NT wood onto a path with houses to the left, and follow it to join an access road. Turn right on the road (Tedgness Road) and descend to the B6521 road.

Cross the road and turn right for 50 metres, then turn left on the path signed 'Station'. This is a tarmac path taking you down to the Grindleford Station. The old station

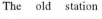

Wellington's Monument near Baslow

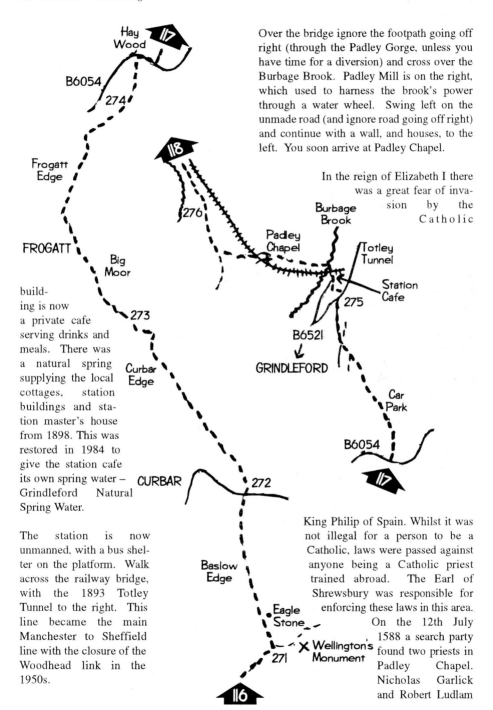

Over the bridge ignore the footpath going off right (through the Padley Gorge, unless you have time for a diversion) and cross over the Burbage Brook. Padley Mill is on the right, which used to harness the brook's power through a water wheel. Swing left on the unmade road (and ignore road going off right) and continue with a wall, and houses, to the left. You soon arrive at Padley Chapel.

In the reign of Elizabeth I there was a great fear of invasion by the Catholic

building is now a private cafe serving drinks and meals. There was a natural spring supplying the local cottages, station buildings and station master's house from 1898. This was restored in 1984 to give the station cafe its own spring water – Grindleford Natural Spring Water.

The station is now unmanned, with a bus shelter on the platform. Walk across the railway bridge, with the 1893 Totley Tunnel to the right. This line became the main Manchester to Sheffield line with the closure of the Woodhead link in the 1950s.

King Philip of Spain. Whilst it was not illegal for a person to be a Catholic, laws were passed against anyone being a Catholic priest trained abroad. The Earl of Shrewsbury was responsible for enforcing these laws in this area.

On the 12th July 1588 a search party found two priests in Padley Chapel. Nicholas Garlick and Robert Ludlam were arrested, and taken to Derby. At their trial they were found guilty and, together with another priest called Richard Simpson, they were hung, drawn and quartered on the 24th July. Since 1898 the chapel has become a place of pilgrimage in memory of the martyrs, who are now officially called 'Blessed'. The chapel was restored in 1933 and is open to the public from the end of

HATHERSAGE

GR SK 232 815

278

Station   A625

277

Leadmill
Bridge

April to the end of September on Sundays and Wednesdays between 2 and 4pm. The ruins of the 1400 Padley Hall lie behind the chapel.

B6001

Beyond the chapel carry on the track for a further 100 metres, then turn left through a gate and bridge over the railway lines. Follow the left wall to the field end. Turn right in the same field to follow the wall, then into the centre of the next field. Cross to prominent gate posts opposite. In the next field bear right to a stile near the railway and into Coppice Wood. This is National Trust property. Carry on the path, and meet another path. Turn right, then meet a track, and turn right again along the bank of the River

River Derwent

Derwent. The NT land is left as you continue along the riverbank. At one point the river swings left and the path cuts across the field to join the river as it swings back again. Pass to the left of Harpur Lees house and go onto its tarmac drive. The drive carries on along the river bank. Sweet Cicely lines the bank. You finally arrive at the B6001 road at Leadmill bridge.

Cross the road and turn half-right to follow the left fence all the way to Nether Hall Lodge and a minor road. Turn left on the road, and pass under the railway viaduct. There is a housing estate to the right. You reach the B6001 road again with The Little John inn to the right. Turn left to Hathersage centre and the A625 road. On your right is an unusual lamppost —

Erected by
Public subscription
in memory of
the late
Col A J Shuttleworth JP
(Retired RA)
of Hathersage Hall
AD 1914

Hathersage is the end of the first 278 miles (445 km) of the Great English Walk. Hathersage has good bus connexions, and has a rail service to both Manchester and Sheffield. The town has connexions with Robin Hood, and especially Little John – but more of that in the second volume.

You have walked through open farmland, moors, climbed hills, perhaps got a little lost in vast fields, walked through a city, and many hamlets and villages. We hope you have enjoyed seeing some of the best scenery that England has to offer, and looking forward to continuing your journey to Berwick-upon-Tweed.

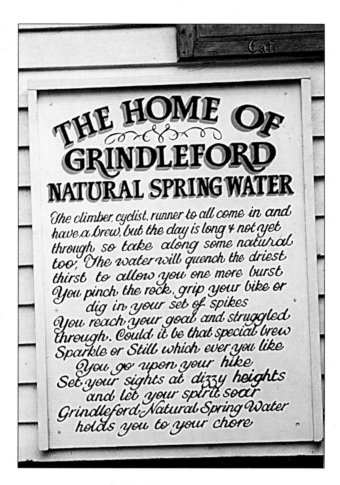

Grindleford Natural Spring Water

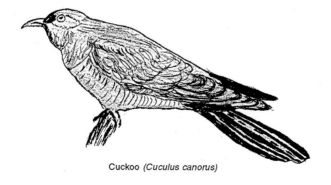

Cuckoo (Cuculus canorus)

Facility List

	Inn	Accomm- odation	PO	Store	Public Conveniences
Chepstow	Y	Y	Y	Y	Y
Aylburton	Y	Y	Y	Y	Y
VineyHill	Y	Y	Y	N	N
Blakeney	Y	Y	Y	Y	Y
Littledean	Y	Y	Y	Y	Y
Clifford's Mesne	Y	N	N	N	N
Newent	Y	Y	Y	Y	Y
Redmarley D'Abitot	Y	N	Y	Y	N
Wynds Point	Y	Y	N	Y	Y
Wyche Cutting	Y	Y	Y	Y	Y
Great Malvern	Y	Y	Y	Y	Y
Alfrick	Y	Y	Y	Y	N
Knightwick	Y	Y	N	N	N
Berrow Green	Y	Y	N	N	N
Martley	Y	Y	Y	Y	N
Great Witley	Y	Y	Y	N	N
TenburyWells	Y	Y	Y	Y	Y
Clee Hill	Y	Y	Y	Y	Y
Longville in the Dale	Y	Y	N	N	N
Church Stretton	Y	Y	Y	Y	Y
Longnor	N	N	Y	Y	N
Dorrington	Y	Y	Y	Y	N
Bayston Hill	Y	N	Y	Y	N
Shrewsbury	Y	Y	Y	Y	Y
Astley	Y	N	N	N	N
Hadnall	Y	Y	Y	Y	N
Grinshill	Y	N	N	N	N
Clive	Y	Y	Y	Y	N
Wem	Y	Y	Y	Y	Y
Whitchurch	Y	Y	Y	Y	Y
Grindley Brook	Y	N	N	N	N
Malpas	Y	Y	Y	Y	N
Tarporley	Y	Y	Y	Y	Y
Wettonhall	Y	N	N	N	N
Church Minshull	Y	Y	Y	Y	N
Warmingham	Y	Y	N	N	N
Brereton Green	Y	Y	Y	Y	N
Astbury	Y	Y	Y	N	N

	Inn	Accomm-odation	PO	Store	Public Conveniences
Congleton	Y	Y	Y	Y	Y
Biddulph (north)	Y	Y	Y	N	Y
Biddulph Town	Y	Y	Y	Y	Y
Biddulph Moor	Y	Y	Y	Y	N
Lask Edge	N	Y	N	N	N
Longsdon	Y	Y	Y	Y	N
Cats Edge	N	Y	N	N	N
Cheddleton	Y	Y	Y	Y	N
Basford Bridge	Y	Y	N	N	N
Waterfall	Y	Y	N	N	N
Waterhouses	Y	Y	Y	Y	Y
Wetton	Y	Y	Y	N	Y
Alstonefield	Y	Y	Y	Y	Y
Hartington	Y	Y	Y	Y	Y
Monyash	Y	Y	Y	Y	Y
Youlgreave	Y	Y	Y	Y	Y
Bakewell	Y	Y	Y	Y	Y
Edensor	N	N	Y	Y	Y
Baslow	Y	Y	Y	Y	Y
Grindleford	Y	Y	Y	Y	N
Leadmills	Y	Y	N	N	N
Hathersage	Y	Y	Y	Y	Y

Redwing *(Turdus iliacus)*

ALTERATIONS TO TEXT   Vol one

Footpath diversions:

P 16   ....shown as Ross farm on the map.   Go 10 metres past the house, then turn right through a stile. Follow the left hedge to the bottom left corner and go through a stile on the left.   Turn half right to cross a field to a gate on the left into a wood.   Turn right and descend a slope to a footbridge and stepping stones over a stream and boggy area.   Climb the field......

p 17......Pass Park Farm and follow the stiles to a stile giving access to a minor road at Nupend.   DON'T CROSS the stile, but turn sharp left and head across the middle of the field..........

p 17   ....then turn right along 'The Gables' drive.   10 metres before reaching the house turn right across several flag stones and through a gate into 'The Gables' garden.   Turn right along the hedge and left at the bottom of the garden, then leave via a stile into a field.   Go diagonally right down the field to reach Church Road.

p 109   ...to a new housing estate.   The path goes left and then right through the estate to cross an estate road.   Leave over a footbridge and stile into a field. Cross half right and into a small green lane.....

p 164..from Lee House keep to right of wall/fence (in trees initially) up hill to cross over a stile and onto a minor road.

p 188..   In 1997 the PO/Store closed in the following Aylburton, Church Minshull(also Inn), Brereton Green.